Education Unleashed

What is the purpose of public education? Writing from his experience as a father, small business owner, and policymaker, Georgia's Lieutenant Governor Casey Cagle presents a comprehensive vision to transform the way that public schools educate our students. Beginning with an idea which unites all Americans—that public education establishes the foundational promise of opportunity for all individuals by empowering us with the ability to learn, develop, and obtain anything we are willing to work for—Cagle makes the case for reforming our schools and rethinking the premise behind how we set and measure goals for student achievement. This is truly the challenge of a generation.

Public schools are important—not just because of the millions of students who will spend thirteen years of their lives learning and preparing for the future in their classrooms—but also for the hundreds of thousands of teachers and educators who spend countless hours each week going above and beyond their duties to make sure all students are able to succeed. Most importantly, the central role of public education includes fostering the strength of our families, communities, and upholding the guiding principles of our nation.

Seeking to remove the obstacles that impede student achievement, while eliminating any justification for complacency in our schools, Cagle explains a thoughtful vision for the future of public education, turning the status quo on its head in favor of leading individual systems, schools, teachers, students, and communities to educational excellence—today and for future generations.

MERCER UNIVERSITY PRESS

Endowed by

TOM WATSON BROWN

and

THE WATSON-BROWN FOUNDATION, INC.

Education Unleashed

Casey Cagle

MERCER UNIVERSITY | MACON, GEORGIA

2016

MUP/ P537

9 8 7 6 5 4 3 2 1

All royalties from the sales of this book will go to The Charter System Foundation's
Educator Leadership Development Program.

Books published by Mercer University Press are printed on acid-
free paper that meets the requirements of the American National
Standard for Information Sciences—Permanence of Paper for
Printed Library Materials.

ISBN   978-0-88146-593-8
Cataloging-in-Publication Data is available from the Library of
Congress

Contents

To my mom, Jeannette

Foreword by

Malcolm Mitchell

Playing football has always felt natural to me. I love being on the field, and will never lose sight of how grateful I am to have been given such a gift. During my time at the University of Georgia, I had to confront the challenge of recovering from an injury. Through that process, I learned the value of patience, persistence, and how important it is to stay passionate about the things I love. Most of all, I learned how to hold on to a dream long enough to see it through. The fact that I have been able to watch my dreams turn into reality—becoming a published author, graduating from college, and moving on to compete with some of the greatest athletes in the world as part of the NFL—has continued to strengthen my determination to help kids realize how much potential they have to make their own mark on the world. Out of all the experiences that have changed my life, nothing has made me as aware of my potential as reading. It has encouraged me to continuously drive myself to improve as a person and take advantage of every available opportunity in order to reach my full potential.

For many athletes, it is easy to watch your identity become so closely associated to your performance on the field that it defines how others see you—and at times, affects the way you think about yourself. There was a period in my life when I felt that way. However, after sustaining a knee injury early in my third year of playing football at the University of Georgia, I started to really look inward and find my true sense of self. Through reading, I discovered a new outlook on life that has expanded my imagination and inspired me to reach out to others. Reading is the foundation for success that can give anyone the ability to accomplish their dreams.

As I grew older and assumed a leadership role with my team, I found myself in the position of offering advice to younger players who weren't always sure of how to best prepare their mindset before going into games. My advice was always the same: never forget that this is football, and the reason you are in a position to play in this game is because you have the talent to succeed on the field. It didn't matter who our opponent was or where we were playing, the best guidance I could ever give to any player was to know that when the moment comes, he would have the ability to make the play. Worrying about some games—or moments—being more important than others would only cause their intensity to fluctuate and make their play inconsistent. As I have become an avid reader, I've learned that the same lesson applies to getting an education and taking advantage of our abilities and surroundings each and every day.

When I wrote my first book, *The Magician's Hat*, I wanted to share one of the most valuable lessons I have learned with as many children as possible. After I began reading at a more advanced level and started to experience the benefits of reading, no matter what else happened in my life, I knew that nothing would ever stop me from reaching my full potential and accomplishing my goals. Like me, Lieutenant Governor Casey Cagle has had experiences in life which have taught him the difference between succumbing to limitations and reaching your goals. This has motivated him to share the benefits of lifelong learning with all students enrolled in Georgia's public school system. I know firsthand that there are many people who are waiting for the spark that will unleash their potential.

Acknowledgments

Serving as Georgia's lieutenant governor is one of the greatest privileges of my life. I will be eternally grateful to the people of my state who have entrusted me with their faith and support.

I am thankful to my family: the love of my life, Nita; my son, Jared, his wife, Kaylan, and my granddaughter, Everett; my son Grant and his wife Meghan; and my son, Carter.

Writing this book has been a journey, and I appreciatively acknowledge that it would not have become a reality without substantial contributions from those around me. Foremost, I want to recognize Danny Kanso, who has been my closest collaborator in writing and producing this book. Danny took on this project with great passion and determination, sharing my goals of wanting to give readers access to the stories and ideas expressed herein. I owe my sincere thanks to Danny for spending countless hours working with me to get this right, and offering his talents to help publish my vision for the future of our public schools. I am grateful to my chief legal counsel, Irene Munn, who has led the way in organizing this effort and assisted further in preparing and editing many drafts. Through this process, I am fortunate to have been advised by Ben Fry. I recognize the leadership of Bo Butler, my chief of staff, whose involvement has been essential to this book's publication. Thank you to Lou Erste, who generously offered his time and expertise. I also acknowledge the work of Jasmine Kidd, who authored her own contribution to this book. I am deeply appreciative of all the individuals who have dedicated a part of their lives in making this book a reality.

Most importantly, I recognize the dedication and hard work put forward by the teachers and educators who work every single day to make our public education system the very best that it can be for all the students who are enrolled in our schools.

Introduction

Intelligence plus character—that is the goal of true education.[1]
—Martin Luther King, Jr.

Public education is not only the greatest core function of government in Georgia, it is also what provides the foundational promise of opportunity to our citizens. All of the students enrolled in every one of our public schools deserve an education that will allow them to obtain the knowledge and skills necessary to accomplish their goals. Since I took office as Georgia's lieutenant governor in 2007, I have focused on offering models of innovation, pathways for choice, and options to expand local collaboration in our state's public schools that will afford students better opportunities to succeed.

I am writing this book because I believe that for too long we have failed to advance a discussion on a statewide level about how to better address the needs of individual public school students and the people who are integral to educating Georgia's children. This book is for students, parents, teachers, principals, business leaders, and everyone in communities across Georgia who have an interest in reforming our education system to reward achievement and to ensure that our students graduate with high school degrees from academically and professionally advanced programs.

Education is the underlying foundation of our society, and America rewards those characteristics that are largely developed during our primary and secondary educations. Attributes like critical thinking, confidence to ask challenging questions, entrepreneurial and innovative mindsets, and an active interest in reading and learning all develop during the thirteen years that our children spend in public schools. We cannot think about our education system in partisan terms or use teachers and students as political footballs because education is more than a two-party issue. In fact, America's greatest domestic challenge may well be to overcome the ideological divisiveness of Washington politics to achieve real education reform nationwide because our hope for the future rests on the promise of our children's success.

Fortunately, we don't need to wait for the federal government to transform education in Georgia. In this book, as I explain my vision for public education, I draw from my experience not only as lieutenant governor, but also as a father and from my career as an entrepreneur. The understanding that I have developed from talking with thousands of Georgians has made me certain of the great opportunity waiting in our future. When we unleash our education system and adjust our outlook to reflect that the education our children receive belongs at the center of our attention in our families and communities, and must, without question, be the focus in every one of our schools, we will address many of our society's most systemic problems and build a stronger Georgia.

Our future means everything to me, and I have always been proud to call Georgia my home. I grew up with a sincere appreciation for the value of community because my family has lived in Hall County for seven generations. Last year, my son Jared and his wife, Kaylan, announced they were expecting their own addition to our family. On October 2, 2015, we welcomed Everett Grace Cagle into the world. On that day, I had a moment of reflection and thought back to how everything has aligned so perfectly for our family that we have been able to call Georgia home for centuries. From that day forward, I started imagining what life is going to be like for my granddaughter and where her future will take our family.

My own future has never been easy to predict. I can say that the most important decision I have ever made occurred more than thirty years ago when, toward the beginning of my senior year at

Johnson High School, I was in the gym and my football coach called me over in one of his efforts to offer some advice. Out of nowhere Coach Woodruff said, "Casey, you need to start dating a good girl." I didn't understand where he was coming from and asked if he was trying to say that I was dating girls who weren't good for me. He responded with authority: "No. I mean a real good girl," and he gestured across the gym and said, "Someone just like Nita over there." I trusted his advice, so I walked over and started talking with Nita.

That next Sunday night, Nita and I went to church together, and a few days later, we started dating. After I bought my first business at twenty-one years old, I proposed to her. The rest is history, and we recently celebrated our twenty-ninth anniversary. I couldn't have imagined back then that taking Coach Woodruff's advice would lead us to where our family is today. Over the following nine years, we had three sons: Jared, Grant, and Carter. My three boys are the pride of my life.

When I was elected to the state Senate, I made a promise to myself that, at night, I would make it a practice to return home to Gainesville—without letting the long commute to Atlanta separate me from my family. I feel that Nita and our boys are my greatest calling in life, and much more so than my experience in politics or business, taking an active role in their lives has enriched mine. Each day I am motivated to work as hard as possible for the 1.7 million public school students in Georgia because I understand that as a parent, there is no reward greater than watching your children achieve success on their own.

In 2006, I was elected to serve as Georgia's lieutenant governor. Since I was sworn into the Senate in 1995, I have watched the conversation shift to what now is a question of how we can meet our paramount and constitutional obligation to provide more than an adequate education for all of the children in the state of Georgia by reforming our public schools from the ground up. We may disagree on how best to provide a system that will allow all of our students to become successful, but it cannot be disputed that—for better or for worse—the quality of our public schools is a critical factor in determining the future of almost every child raised in our state. In good conscience, we can no longer kick the can down the road because our children cannot afford to wait any longer for us to improve their schools. This book is my attempt to bring concerns voiced by countless parents, teachers, and business leaders about the future of Georgia's children to the forefront of our attention as we look towards the comprehensive process of education reform that will positively transform our state's future.

I want to share my vision for what our public education system could be and what we must diligently work to achieve. I want to challenge our state to adopt a new mindset in which we view education as the central driver of growth and forward progress for individuals, communities, and statewide economic development. Hundreds of thousands of educators in the state of Georgia dedicate their lives to teaching our students because they want to make the world a better place—and they answer to a higher calling in their careers. We have to give all of our teachers the ability to educate each student to the full extent of his or her ability.

Debate on how to most effectively reform education is healthy, and it is imperative to have a collaborative discussion to find a solution to this complex policy issue. This book is my contribution to that debate. I recognize that there will be disagreement with my vision for public education, but it is vital for the future of our children that we have an honest debate. Without exception, the ideas that I will present are based on the principle that the success of tomorrow depends on the education that our children receive today.

1

Defining Success in Public Education

Education is the most powerful weapon which you can use to change the world.[2]

—Nelson Mandela

Outside of the rights and liberties granted under the United States Constitution, public education is the greatest equalizer among people in our society. No matter your social background or where you are from, education gives every person the opportunity to earn a better life. Education gives us the possibility of turning our dreams into reality—every astronaut, doctor, lawyer, plumber, or electrician has developed the foundation of his or her life through education. In this book, when I discuss my vision for public education in Georgia, I will define "adequate education" as graduating from high school with the knowledge and skills required to be either college-ready or directly employable. Moreover, the objectives of our state's public education system should be greater than for our schools simply to promote students to the next grade level, to meet certain standardized testing averages, or to issue a greater number of status quo high school diplomas.

It is no longer possible to rationalize and accept the current operations of Georgia's public education system, with almost every school educating its students the same way and with a top-down decision-making process that constrains the abilities of teachers in classrooms across our state. Georgia's public schools are not alone in their need for reform, but instead of seeking top-down federal legislation, I believe that the only way we can improve the quality of our children's education is by restructuring our statewide public education system to empower local leaders, principals, and teachers with significant decision-making authority. Working under the direction of school-level leaders, the Department of Education and local school boards could more effectively contribute to, and support the efforts of, Georgia's 2,300 schools to move beyond the specific challenges faced by their students each school year.[3]

America is an exceptional nation, in part, because we have accepted the responsibility of providing everyone in our society with the opportunity to succeed by obtaining an education in our public schools. I believe that the state of Georgia has a five-year window to meet the challenge of comprehensive public education reform. If we fail to offer a better future for students, we will lose the momentum that our state has generated and forfeit the remarkable opportunities waiting in our future.

I am confident, however, that we will be successful. In the future, opportunities for Georgians will be driven upward because of our ability to deliver a world-class education to a diverse society that is growing alongside an ever-changing economy. To introduce my vision for the future of public education, I will outline ten principles that I believe our schools must embrace to offer the educational outcomes our students deserve.

1. Abandon the One-Size-Fits-All System

For our public schools to shift their attention from following mandates to accomplishing achievement-based goals, we have to adopt a new mindset. My vision for public education requires that every school system in Georgia commits to raising expectations for students in two ways: First, our schools must establish an academic floor with no cracks that ensures students do not get left behind academically or drop out of school—which will demand a 100 percent graduation rate. Second, both primary and secondary schools have to be given the freedom and flexibility to lift arbitrary performance ceilings that force more consideration to be given to a student's age than to his or her academic ability. There is no room for system-wide one-size-fits-all policies under my vision for the future of our public schools.

In districts statewide, it is critical for our schools to adopt new models of management and administrative operations that allow the Department of Education and local school boards to more effectively coordinate. An interviewer once asked Michael Horn, co-author of the book *Disrupting Class*, "If you could give one educational tool to every child in the world, what would it be? Why?" Horn replied, "The ability to learn at the pace and path that makes sense for each student, not for the system. We all have different learning needs at different times. One tool won't fix this—and thinking it will is misguided; students need access to many tools, but mostly we need to unlock them from a world in which time is fixed and learning is variable."[4] From kindergarten to twelfth grade, we are making too many decisions automatically for students. To the greatest extent possible, we should empower our students and parents to make choices, explore different academic areas, and individually determine the best path forward to accomplish their goals after graduating from high school.

2. Teachers and Principals are Essential

Teachers understand the needs of students better than anyone. Principals understand the needs of teachers better than anyone. A good principal is capable of attracting, hiring, and retaining good teachers to educate each school's students. Unfortunately, we often marginalize input from our teachers and principals because we already have a set of "experts" who are in control of managing our school systems. This mentality is extremely damaging. Teachers understand what each individual student needs to learn, in what areas he or she is deficient, and his or her potential for greatness. Principals provide teachers with the support they need to effectively serve their students. When our teachers and principals are truly free to meet the educational needs of students, we will be able to achieve excellence in every single classroom. No one achieves success alone. To provide all of our students with the educations they deserve, we have to restructure our public education system to give principals, teachers, and supporting faculty the freedom to perform to the best of their abilities.

School districts across Georgia should be empowered with the freedom and flexibility to formulate reform measures that will drive better outcomes. We should stop blaming our teachers for what they are unable to control due to the fact that we prevent them from having authority over how to best instruct their students. Removing many of the mandates and obstacles, which force our teachers to spend much of their time in the classroom preparing students for standardized tests that often unfairly or unreliably measure performance, will go a long way toward giving educators the value and input they deserve. When we adjust the tools that we use to assess student performance, we can also bring greater accountability into our public schools by allowing districts to fairly evaluate the performance of their teachers formatively—based on the job duties they fulfill day in and day out—rather than using the same high stakes summative assessments that are failing our students.

To maximize the potential for our educators, they must be a part of the decision-making process, formulating the methods used for evaluation and prescribing the criteria to improve student performance and achievement. An inclusive environment which equips those who work closest alongside our students with instructional authority will change the culture inside our classrooms and help our schools to abandon top-down systems. We can then go further and empower local leaders to turn their attention to easing the burdens placed on educators through a wide range of nonteaching responsibilities—such as supervising lunches and bus routes. In the same respect, those teachers who do more should be fairly and justly compensated individually as opposed to through a one-size fits all tenure pay scale. This is because a structured pay scale gives no recognition to the considerable differences in school districts across our state and, furthermore, cannot distinguish between the different job duties each teacher performs inside and outside of the classroom. Our statewide pay scale should serve as a base, which local districts are able to increase and add different incentives to depending on a variety of factors that recognize the professionalism and respect the work of each individual teacher. We need to explore the array of options in which educators may find value. Some may prefer salary increases, but just as many may desire professional development, expanded planning time, greater job sharing opportunities, enhanced work environments, and upgraded technologies to utilize in their classrooms. Some will benefit from other locally developed programs. We will find success in education when we value our teachers by making sure they are equipped with the best resources and compensated monetarily and professionally.

Irrespective of any reforms that may be enacted, I am committed to making sure that the state of Georgia honors the promises made to current and retired educators. Meeting our obligations to these individuals is the least we can do.

Education already maintains a central role in our lives, but when we give our schools the ability to operate freely, we will unleash a powerful force that will benefit students and their families, unlocking a new wave of potential in communities across Georgia. When we pay teachers fairly and allow each school to make the decisions that only it can assess, we will adopt a new mindset in which teachers are not simply employees of the government, but are truly valued as educators who shape the lives of every student who walks into their classrooms.

3. Define Success Using Measurable Outcomes

Offering a clear definition to quantify success is an inherently necessary aspect of any endeavor and is particularly crucial in public education. Success in public education reform means empowering our school systems to challenge the status quo and to comprehensively rebuild their internal governance structures based on individually defined goals. Above all, we must distinguish between "teaching to the test" and truly measuring academic success in ways that prepare students for lifelong learning.

First, local school districts must outline a vision that includes priorities for their communities, schools, and students. Once a plan of action to measure success is in place, then teachers, principals, and supporting faculty in each school can work collaboratively to establish a roadmap for how to improve their students' academic performance.

For example, if a system's general vision for primary school students is to graduate them from the fifth grade proficient in reading, writing, math, science, and social studies—then that is the goal to which each school's leaders must measure success. To continue along this example, if under Georgia's College and Career Ready Performance Index (CCRPI) 70% of students meet this goal—then that school's leaders must question which steps are necessary to draw a roadmap that can lead all students to achieve proficiency in these basic subjects. Using measurable outcomes to define progress toward each student's goals is extremely important. Ultimately, districts should make decisions on which assessments they use to quantify progress toward reaching their goals. They should then go a step further and establish a clear vision for how each school's operations can be targeted to elevate all students to reach these goals.

While we must set benchmarks for academic achievement at every level, we should never attempt to limit the potential of our students by standardizing the way that we define success within a narrow system of measurement. Success in public education is never going to mean yielding an identical outcome for every single student.

As a society, we should celebrate all types of work and the training required for them. For some students, success will be defined by becoming a building contractor or a mechanic. For other students success will be defined by earning a degree from a college or university and moving into a chosen career field. We need to make sure that we do everything possible to offer all our students access to different models of education that can help them fulfill their ambitions. I believe that the purpose of our public education system is to provide individuals with the knowledge, skills, and experience needed to be either college-bound or career-ready and immediately employable upon graduating from high school.

Measuring Success: Georgia's College and Career Ready
*   Performance Index (CCRPI)[5]*

Statewide, academic progress in our schools is measured annually using Georgia's College and Career Readiness Performance Index (CCRPI). Georgia first implemented CCRPI after the state received a 2012 federal waiver from the assessment requirements of No Child Left Behind. The CCRPI index measures student academic performance in language arts, mathematics, science, and social studies using assessments, as well as readiness to advance from elementary, middle, and high school.

In 2014, out of 100 possible points, Georgia's schools registered averages of 72.7 in elementary schools, 73.8 in middle schools, and 68.4 in high schools.[6] CCRPI is a tool that has improved our ability to measure the performance of Georgia's schools, and it is incumbent upon us to continue working to improve how we measure success in our schools. I believe that school districts across our state should use the progress made by CCRPI as a starting place to develop innovative measures of academic performance that allow them to break outside of the status quo in favor of reaching new heights academically for their students. Each of our schools must ask: *What is our strategic plan to improve each and every year so that our students can achieve better results?* We need to continue to bring together a variety of tools to determine how well our schools are preparing students for careers and life after graduating from high school.

4. Establish a Governance Structure to Make Decisions Closest to Students

Shifting decision-making authority down from the State Board of Education to local school boards and to principals and governing councils will empower individuals at every level to accept personal responsibility for transforming our public education system. Allowing each school system to implement the best possible management structure to fit the needs of its students is the central tenet of the most forward-looking education reform in the nation: charter systems.

Since the Charter Systems Act was signed into law in 2007, charter systems have been among the most successful schools in the state of Georgia. Charter systems empower schools to take responsibility for their students and incorporate teachers, parents, and communities into the public education system. A school system's success cannot be mandated from a central office. But when every school district is given the ability to establish its own budget and operational structure without federal or state mandates, each of its schools quickly becomes a distinctive institution, rather than just another building where students are zoned in from a larger system. Freedom, ownership, and innovation are the essential properties that teachers and principals are able to develop in their schools with independent decision-making authority.

WHAT IS A CHARTER SYSTEM?[7]

Charter systems give schools freedom from following most state regulations and mandates in exchange for improving student academic performance under an accountability contract made between the State Board of Education and a local school district. As charter systems, districts receive flexibility to operate within a general set of parameters in return for accepting greater accountability over their students' educational outcomes.

All charter systems place a direct emphasis on school-based leadership and decision-making, authorizing local governance teams to make decisions on employment practices and budget outlays, and to write a strategic plan that reforms curricula, instruction, and daily operations. Local governance teams include parents, teachers and faculty, community members, principals, and high school students and can be uniquely structured to accommodate any other stakeholders who contribute value to our schools.

It is important to understand that charter systems operate very differently than stand alone charter schools. Charter systems require participation and engagement from entire school districts to convert their operations into localized models, structured to positively transform the communities in which they operate—leaving no one behind. By empowering systems as a whole to deliver upon locally developed strategic plans for a quality-based education, charter systems are unleashing powerful agents of growth and development into communities throughout Georgia.

5. Write an Accountability Contract

The central component that has enabled many of our state's charter systems to improve the academic performance of students is the fact that these districts are required to outline their goals—and the metrics by which they will be evaluated—in an accountability contract. Initial accountability contracts are issued for five years, and can then be renewed for another ten years. In these contracts, schools articulate a strategic plan to reach their goals for student achievement. Accountability contracts do not have to be exclusive to charter systems, and can have a similarly positive impact under other governance structures.

Rather than simply carrying out the functions of a standard business contract—outlining things such as how many days students will attend classes and how leaders will govern— accountability contracts provide much greater value by serving as a road map that guides each school to individually determine its own destiny. Accountability contracts give districts the opportunity to redesign the public education system to better fit each community. Imagine if our schools were fortified to address the problems that students most frequently struggle with. Or, conversely: *What if public schools personalized their operations and utilized the value of businesses and postsecondary institutions within their communities?* The results would be extraordinary.

Accountability contracts enable the stakeholders in each school district to join together to present a clear and positive vision for the future of students. By bringing together different resources in each community to strengthen elementary, middle, and high schools, accountability contracts empower students to take advantage of the quality of their schools by making personal investments to participate in programs and activities. Consider this analogy: Rather than utilizing an expensive landscaping service, homeowners are, instead, given the option of buying any variety of lawnmower that best suits their needs. With a lawnmower of their own, homeowners can cut their grass whenever they feel like it, instead of relying on a landscaping service to cut it at fixed intervals. Despite the initial outlay of the price of the lawnmower, the homeowner would still see financial savings over time. When individuals are given the freedom to make their own choices in return for taking accountability for the results, it becomes possible to define a floor for minimum expectations without also establishing a ceiling that limits potential outcomes.

An accountability contract individually redefines each school's purpose, and most importantly, gives every educator direction and a mandate to focus on achievement and innovation. When all of our schools begin with these goals in mind—focusing on the end result of educating our students to reach the highest academic level possible—then teachers, principals, parents, students, and our communities can take responsibility for the outcomes.

6. Give Schools Ownership

Throughout every consequential period of American history, people have found solutions to overcome obstacles and have grown to reach new heights. Regarding the growth that Georgia has experienced during the past century, there is an observable pattern in our history that demonstrates our capacity to stretch and achieve something better when we confront serious challenges. The implementation of school-level decision-making, and the empowering of teachers, principals, and local leaders to design operating structures and budgets to support them will bring the benefits of free enterprise into our public schools.

During my first campaign for state Senate, I was visiting a barbeque in Oconee County when a voter approached me to strike up a conversation. After we talked for a few minutes, I told him that it would be my honor to receive his vote. He replied that he had only one question to ask me: "When you sign your checks, do you sign the front or the back?" What he was really asking me was if I had to meet a payroll and make the tough decisions that went along with being an employer—or if someone else signed my paycheck. I told him I sign my checks on the front, and he responded that I had his vote. This gentleman didn't mean to demean other people who are employed, but wanted to know if I could be a leader and make the tough choices needed to move our state forward.

Throughout my career, both publically and privately, I've had to make tough choices. As Georgia's lieutenant governor, I have to, on a daily basis, prioritize what is essential and what is non-essential. In my opinion, there is nothing more essential to the future well being of our state than public education.

Freed from the micromanagement of daily operations by the state and federal governments, our public schools can begin to view themselves as unique entities. This will bring school systems closer to our communities. Each school cannot be viewed as part of the state educational bureaucracy, but rather must be recognized as an integral part of each community. Individuals at every level of public education—especially those closest to students—have to be empowered with the decision-making authority necessary to take ownership over the educational outcomes delivered by our schools. In a similar respect, when more opportunities are available to students, our schools can create an environment in which greater accountability is required of them. Giving students the ability to take advantage of new opportunities, such as industry certifications, will allow them to distinctly see value in the education they receive to equip them with marketable skills that lead to well-paying jobs. In return, educators should be able to expect their students to become more engaged. Our objective is to bring meaning and purpose into public schools so that each student finds the value that will motivate him or her to accept greater accountability.

7. Offer Freedom and Flexibility

Just as each student is different, so too is every school, teacher, and classroom. We cannot offer our students access to individualized learning plans until we give school systems the power to budget their resources as effectively as possible. Instead of imposing compliance-based mandates, our primary focus should be encouraging schools to innovate so they can improve their students' performance. In addition to managing day-to-day operations, schools should also be given the freedom to design their curricula in the way that best meets the needs of individual students.

By allowing every school to make the best decisions for its students, without penalty, and with support from county and statewide offices, we can build much more effective models of innovation from the ground up out of individual public schools. Free enterprise, positive incentives, and innovative ideas have continued to drive growth in our nation's economy up to the present day, and these same principles can be applied effectively in our public education system. When all of Georgia's schools are empowered with the freedom and flexibility to innovate in their own right, teachers will be able to advance new programs without having to wait for top-down approval—and new models of innovation can develop fully without being convoluted by outside interference or bureaucratic intransigence.

8. Education Drives the Economy

Above all, to grow a more dynamic economy, we have to invest in education. If we build an education system that aligns academic achievement to meet the needs of our twenty-first century economy, we will make an investment in Georgia's future that offers a return greater than could anything else.

Companies often decide where to locate based on the quality of public schools and workforce training. Nations, states, and cities that produce the best workforces are the most successful globally. Unfortunately, as a society we haven't focused—to the extent necessary—on developing a modern workforce. In recent decades, our education system hasn't placed a strong enough focus on strategically supporting the workforce development demands necessary to take full advantage of our rapid economic growth.

If we want more manufacturing industries to locate in Georgia, we need to prepare our students with the specific skills for jobs that these industries need to fill, in areas such as welding, engineering, robotics, and computer science. If we want to develop a world-class healthcare system, we need to give more students a foundation in science and math that will encourage them to continue on to a career in healthcare. For Georgia to sustain a leading global economy, our state has to offer students more opportunities to develop knowledge, skills, and experience.

There are countless examples of excellent public schools that already exist in Georgia. In Dublin, schools started offering the International Baccalaureate program in order to encourage overseas companies to locate in their city.[8] College and Career Academies are critical to developing industry in Georgia because they can match their classes to fit the needs of local businesses. The more offerings our schools are able to provide students, the more prosperous our communities will grow.

What is a College and Career Academy?[9]

The mission of all College and Career Academies is to advance workforce development by partnering one or more local boards of education, alongside one or more postsecondary institutions. College and Career Academies strive to increase high school graduation rates, create new career paths and develop educational opportunities to prepare students to be successful both in college, and professionally in careers after graduating from high school.

9. Reward Achievement

If we allocate funding for public education based on compliance with mandates from the state and federal government, a culture of compliance will continue to persist. Teachers often have to challenge the status quo to innovate, and top-down management structures can make it difficult for them to give individual students extra attention without making additional personal sacrifices.

The negative consequences of mandate-based management are the same in both education and business. An examination of the best practices in industry surveyed by Gallup, concluded: "The best workplaces give their employees a sense of purpose, help them feel they belong, and enable them to make a difference."[10] Everyone agrees that teachers are integral to educating the students in our schools, but if we continue to treat educators as contractors, we will further limit our students' ability to realize greatness. When we allow individual schools to reward educators and encourage them to innovate, we can defeat the complacency that exists in our education system and embrace a culture of achievement.

Our society is built around the notion that if someone works hard, they can live with purpose and earn something great. That is the American Dream. My vision for public education is based upon the idea that in addition to recognizing the dignity of work and securing a better future for our children, public education is integral to the success of families, communities, and society as a whole.

10. Our Future is Our Purpose:

Education gives every person access to our dynamic economy. It provides individuals with the building blocks to find and develop their purpose. In order to pursue a successful future, people have to feel a sense of meaning. Our challenge in public education reform is not to find agreement on the mission of educating all of our children—that mission is obvious and imperative. Instead, our challenge is to transform public education outside of the boundaries of a one-size-fits-all system so that each of our schools can follow through to advance every one of its students.

Every child is motivated and challenged in different ways. As the father of three boys, I understand how different individuals can be. We have to design an education system around the needs of each student. I want to challenge the state of Georgia to imagine a system in which our students are working to extend their educations instead of fighting to get out of school. As we continue our process of reform, we have to abandon our assumptions and chart a new course that affords each school the ability to make adjustments in pursuit of academic excellence for all of its students.

2

The American Dream

All our dreams can come true if we have the courage to pursue them.[11]

—Walt Disney

For seven generations, my family has called Hall County home. Despite being only fifty miles north of Atlanta, I have always thought of our home as part of rural Georgia. Growing up, I didn't have an easy childhood. But I was blessed with opportunities to work hard, which enabled me to gain the skills that I would need later in life. My father left my mother when I was three years old, and she raised me herself. Our family faced many difficult times when I was a kid, and to this day, I remember a lot of lessons that I learned the hard way.

Because my family never had much, I developed a personal understanding of the value of accepting every available opportunity to work. My mother was a caring person, and she always put her children ahead of herself and made sure that we had everything we needed. She worked two jobs and never took a dime of public assistance because she said she didn't need it. My mom made tremendous sacrifices and instilled many of my deepest held values: a love of God, the value of hard work, and the importance of perseverance. Despite her hard work, even the money from her two jobs was barely enough to make ends meet, and we had no choice but to move around constantly.

By the time I reached the sixth grade, I had attended eight different elementary schools. We eventually settled in the southern end of Hall County, and my mom was remarried to a wonderful man, George Liotta, who has been a positive role model for me.

Things started to stabilize for our family, and I attended South Hall Middle School and graduated from Johnson High School. Knowing that there was no safety net for me as a kid, I took jobs cutting grass and working chores for our neighbors to earn money. I never had the mindset that it would be impossible to overcome the circumstances that my family faced. In the years since, I have been able to experience the American Dream to its fullest because of the sacrifices my mother made for me, the greatness of opportunity in America, and by working whenever I was offered a job.

I include this chapter to explain why my foundation—in my childhood as I grew up, in the decisions that my wife Nita and I made for our three boys Jared, Grant, and Carter, who all attended public schools, in my service in the state Senate and as Georgia's lieutenant governor—is all grounded in my belief in the value of education, honest work, and perseverance. By advancing public education reform, encouraging entrepreneurship, and to the greatest possible extent allowing them to be combined that we can build a system that allows our students to achieve unprecedented success.

MY STORY:
EARNING THE AMERICAN DREAM IN GEORGIA

When I was in high school, my dream was to play college football. During my senior year, I was recruited to visit colleges, but straightaway, as a defensive back and strong safety, coaches repeatedly told me that I was competing for a limited number of spots with a lot of exceptional athletes. Many plainly said they didn't need me. As time went on, I didn't receive any legitimate offers, and, out of necessity, I started to plan for a future without football.

One morning in May, our home phone rang. When I picked it up and answered, Coach Erk Russell was on the other end of the line. He introduced himself and said, "Casey, I only have one question to ask you: *Are you going to come to Georgia Southern?*" I was caught off guard by his directness. I remember it vividly now, but at the time, I wasn't sure if I had heard Coach Russell correctly. Maybe there was a letter in the mail that hadn't arrived yet. So I responded by telling him that I would love nothing more than to come to Georgia Southern. Then I asked if he had anything to offer me.

Coach Russell told me he was impressed with my visit earlier that year. Then he added: "I'll be honest with you. We don't have a whole lot of money. But let's not worry about money. Let's just get you down here because I want you to play for me." Immediately and out of nowhere, my future clearly presented itself, and I regained confidence that I would be playing college football after all. I committed to Georgia Southern and started practicing with the team in the summer of 1984. At that time, Erk Russell was already a legend in my mind. Going forward from an incredibly successful seventeen-year career as the defensive coordinator for the Georgia Bulldogs, Coach Russell took control of Georgia Southern's modest football program in 1982. At that moment, he started to transform Georgia Southern's program, and led his teams to upset the traditional precedent of national athletics in what many observers have since characterized as a college football miracle.

I don't know exactly what qualities Erk Russell saw in me that made him extend a late offer to join his team. But he always emphasized that when he recruited players, the measure of a person's will to fight was more important than physical size in determining how successful a player could become. Every day, Coach Russell made it clear that our goal—both as individuals and as a unit—was to win a national championship. Each week, we all knew our individual objectives and what we needed to practice together. If anyone forgot, he could plan to receive a personal reminder from Coach Russell and a new set of exercises that he would be certain to remember. Our team viewed every practice and every game as another collaborative step toward fulfilling our pursuit to win a national championship.

In my first year at Georgia Southern, Coach Russell decided to redshirt me so that I could grow as a player and assume a starting position in the future. Soon, however, I found out that I wouldn't get to apply my training to help my team win a national championship. In my first season at Georgia Southern, I tore my Achilles tendon during a routine practice. There was no big play, and no other player was at fault. My body just landed the wrong way on the field, and when I tried to get back up, I couldn't.

I might have been able to recover and eventually earn a starting position on the team roster, but I recognized that, in reality, there was almost no chance my career would involve playing football on Sundays. I was paying my way through school by working and taking out student loans. I knew that it wouldn't be feasible for me to sustain a major injury as a student athlete if it meant taking out more loans and losing valuable time. My highest priority had to be planning for a career. After giving the decision a lot of thought and talking it over with my mom, I moved back to Gainesville.

Even though I was a student at Georgia Southern for less than a year, the experiences that I gained changed the course of my life. Erk Russell was a great coach because he had an extraordinary ability to motivate his players. Far beyond football, and true to his reputation of having an incredible, strategic way of thinking both on and off the field, Coach Russell made a considerable impact on my life. He helped me become conscious of my ability to take control over how I spent my life. More than anyone else I remember, Coach Russell inspired people to work as hard as they could. He always found a way to get people to do things they didn't think they were capable of doing—and that had an effect on all of us. The only way to describe it is to say that he taught me the difference, which I know today, between limits and goals.

When I returned home, I enrolled in Gainesville College and started working a part-time job at the Northeast Georgia Racquet Club. I quickly adjusted back to life in Gainesville, and my job at the athletic club gave me an opportunity to regularly network with business people in our community. One of the people I befriended was Charlie Brown. We got to know each other well at the fitness center. On what seemed like an ordinary day, we struck up a conversation, and Charlie told me that he was planning to move into a new career in the music industry.

Previously, Charlie confided in me that he had a passion for writing country music. He told me that it was always his dream to move to Nashville so that he could practice what he loved. Charlie said that because his success as a small-business owner now afforded him the ability to pursue his dream, he was going to jump at the opportunity with everything he had. I started to wish him luck and congratulate him, but before I could get out a full sentence, he asked me if I knew anyone who might be interested in managing his business when he moved beyond his day-to-day role. I answered by asking what kind of person he had in mind. He said, "Someone just like you." Charlie was serious. And after he made the suggestion that I could potentially manage his business, I asked if he wanted to have lunch and talk about it. We agreed to continue our conversation later that week.

When we met, Charlie began to tell me he wanted nothing more than to become a country music singer and songwriter. He admitted that his mind kept wandering back to what it would be like to live his dream, and almost uncontrollably—in the sense that he didn't want to, and for all practical purposes he didn't need to—he couldn't put his energy into doing anything else for any longer. Now, Charlie said, he finally had the financial resources to do what he wanted. Looking across the table, I saw someone who was determined to take whatever risks were necessary to pursue what he believed was his purpose in life. We agreed that day to an arrangement, in which I would work as an apprentice under Charlie Brown's supervision to learn the operational aspects of his business. I also did a little research and concluded that I could work full time as the store's manager and still balance going to Gainesville College—if I took one class in the morning and two classes at night until I finished my degree. Until he determined that I was ready to manage the store on my own, I would work under Charlie's direction and training.

After about six months, Charlie asked me if I would be interested in buying Jean's Bridal and Tux of Class from him outright. He told me that he had made arrangements to move to Nashville and would be leaving Gainesville in a few weeks. Charlie said he thought that I was perfectly capable of being just as successful as he had been. Without hesitating, I told him I would do anything possible to buy the tuxedo shop if we could find a way to make it work. Charlie offered to sell me the store under an owner-financing agreement with very fair terms, if I could manage to put down a small deposit. We did the math together, and set up a payment plan, which gave me a viable path to owning my own business at twenty-one years old. Charlie knew my family wasn't wealthy, and in hindsight it seems obvious that he was going out of his way to give me a once-in-a-lifetime opportunity to realize my dreams too. When I examined his business model, however, I saw that the numbers worked. And I genuinely believed in the potential of the community-oriented approach that he applied to operating Jean's Bridal and Tux of Class.

But there was one factor in the sale we somehow overlooked. Charlie's sister Jean Potter owned the bridal section of the store, and he was responsible for the menswear. When Charlie told Jean he would be moving to Nashville in a matter of weeks and that I was going to become the new owner of the menswear department, she decided that it made sense for her to move on as well, and Jean agreed to sell her business under the same terms of our earlier agreement. At that point in time, if someone asked me what I wanted to pursue professionally, I would have told them that I was studying business to become an entrepreneur, and that my dream was to own and operate a sporting goods store. But after working with Charlie at Jean's Bridal and Tux of Class, I felt like I understood the formalwear business too—and I liked it. I told my mom and step-dad about the opportunity Charlie Brown was offering me. Without hesitating, they told me that if he was willing to owner-finance the store and I needed a down payment to give Charlie, they would take out a second mortgage on their house to provide the money for me to get started.

Before I could stop to comprehend the gravity of what I was getting into, I became the owner of Jean's Bridal and Tux of Class. Not only did my mom and step-dad take out a second mortgage on their home to help me purchase the store, they also contributed to making it a family business by working alongside me. About six months after I bought the store, George joined me full time to help the business gain financial security. Within one year, my mom was working with us too. Not long after that, Nita completed our team. We developed a collaborative operating system and started to gain a larger network of regular customers. Eventually, we opened a second location in Athens. My mom and George took over the Gainesville store, and Nita and I moved to manage the Athens location.

Aside from how fortunate I was to meet Charlie Brown, who enabled me to operate the business model he made successful, I also realize that I was blessed to work with my family. Sharing the rewards of hard work with the people I cared about most, especially as part of my first entrepreneurial endeavor, was an indescribably fulfilling experience. Owning and operating my first business taught me countless lessons about life: I learned what it meant to offer a service to the public, and how to satisfy customer demands—particularly in the bridal industry, where perfection is the expectation and is defined very differently depending on the individual bride. I also learned a lot about business from making a constant effort to better position our store so we could satisfy consumer demand that wasn't being met.

More generally, I gained an understanding of how to run a business and promote a vision for a product that is subject to success or failure based on the will of consumers. My business's future was directly dependent on my ability to leave a positive impression with the people whom I was serving. In addition to providing a stable income, which gave Nita and I the ability to prepare our home with everything our new and growing family needed, we also saved up a large enough portion of our earnings to make new investments.

I made it a habit to frequently ask my friends questions about their businesses and financial investments. I wanted to know the secret to other people's success so I could become successful too.

Growing up, one of my best friends was Tommy Gay. He came from a well-off family, and I thought they had everything. I remember when we were young, we used to play beside a gigantic dish perched in his backyard that gave his house access to satellite television—a rare privilege at that time in North Georgia. Tommy also had a very nice boat in a private dock right behind his house on Lake Lanier, which gave us untold hours of entertainment. Despite his family's wealth, I still remember Tommy as one of the most down-to-earth, practical people I have ever known. It never felt like we were very different from one another, even though we had almost opposite economic foundations.

Tommy's father, Dallas, was one of the most successful people I had ever met. I admired Dallas not just for the money he made, but more so for all of the positive things he did in our community. I will never forget what he said to me as a sixteen-year-old kid, when I asked him to tell me the secret to his success. I listened intently for an answer after I finally got around to asking him that question, which had been on my mind for some time. I expected that whatever Dallas would tell me I could apply to myself. When he responded by gazing up at the sky and saying, "Casey, I'll tell you the secret," I was so excited.

After pausing for a minute, he said: "Buy low. Sell high." I was admittedly disappointed with his short answer, and we both laughed about it. But as I reflect on my experience as an entrepreneur, I realize that Dallas was right, and it was some of the best advice I've been given. In every business I have invested in, we created value by keeping expenses at the lowest possible level and producing something that appreciated to sell for a profit. It has been my experience in both government and business, that it is very difficult to predict exactly what your revenues will amount to, and there is always uncertainty despite your best efforts to make well-informed estimates and predictions. However, there is much greater certainty in your ability to control expenses.

When the Great Recession hit Georgia, it affected our state deeply. We had to cut $3.5 billion in spending from our state budget. [12] I knew from my experience in business that we needed to determine exactly what we were going to cut—and make those difficult decisions immediately because that would be the only way to stop the bleeding. Only then, could we readjust our focus and help people build themselves back up from what was near economic ruin for hundreds of thousands of Georgians. We couldn't go backwards and reverse the economic downturn, but we could look forward and build a stronger economic foundation for the future. Because we were able to cut much of the waste that existed in state government, we were better positioned to invest our state's increasing revenue collections into the core areas of public education, infrastructure, and meeting our obligations in governing the state.

The most significant benefit I gained from operating my first business was an early infusion of capital, which gave me the opportunity to reach for a new level of success as an entrepreneur. A few years into owning my business, we were performing consistently well enough that I felt comfortable hiring a capable staff to take over the store's daily operations. I took Dallas's advice seriously, and I wanted to invest in assets that were positioned to gain value and attract a significant increase in demand in the future.

J.L. Yopp, our pastor when Nita and I lived in south Hall County and went to Westside Baptist Church, was an astute investor and owned a few properties he rented to families in Hall County. We were good friends, and when I told him that I wanted to use my formalwear stores as leverage to invest in other business opportunities, he started describing the investments he was making in rental properties. Pastor Yopp explained that he first saw the opportunity when he observed a potentially profitable relationship between property values and average rental prices in Hall County. Then he told me about how he acquired and financed his investments—without taking on more than he could manage— and explained why he felt as though well-placed investments in rental property in Hall County offered a great potential return. In fact, J.L. said that he had just received a tip a few days earlier about a property he was going to look at the following day. He asked me to go with him to see the house, and as a twenty-six-year-old who had just recently been introduced to the many draws of entrepreneurship, I excitedly agreed.

When we looked at the house, J.L. said he thought it was being offered for a more-than fair price and would be a great first property investment. I trusted his judgment, and the house seemed appealing enough, so I went to the bank, and my application to finance the property under a short-term mortgage was approved. Within a couple of months, I accepted an offer to sign a one-year lease to rent the house. Taking Pastor Yopp's advice, I used most of the money that was generated to pay down the principle on the property's mortgage. About three years after I purchased the house, I was reviewing my loan statement and preparing to write another check for a monthly payment, when I stopped to observe how low the mortgage's balance was getting. At that point, I realized that, in a relatively short period—from the time that I acquired this asset until now—the person who was renewing their lease to rent my property was essentially purchasing this asset.

I thought back to J.L.'s advice, and recognized that he had been 100 percent right. From that point forward, I made a conscious effort to start acquiring new income-producing rental properties. The cumulative return from the entrepreneurial endeavors I invested in made it possible for me to start my most personally rewarding business in 1998, when I put together a group of investors to capitalize Southern Heritage Bank.

Despite today's elected majority, Georgia does not have a long history of voting to support Republican officeholders. In 1994, I was the first Republican elected to represent Hall County in the state Senate in more than a century. I am the first—and only—Republican lieutenant governor in Georgia's history. There is a stereotypical view that many Republicans are born into wealthy families and, as a result, don't have an understanding of the challenges faced by families who are financially insecure. I can assure you that my life story has been the opposite experience. Voters have trusted me to govern because I have worked to advance policy priorities that offer increased opportunity, choice, and access to resources so that more Georgians can work to become self-sufficient, successful, and employed in meaningful careers.

In 1994, as a twenty-eight-year-old entrepreneur without any real political experience, I decided to run against an established incumbent Democrat to represent Hall and Forsyth counties in Georgia's fifty-six member Senate. As I managed my business over several years, I started to feel as though the procedures I had to follow to legally comply with government regulations were so duplicative and time-consuming that there had to be a better way to do things. What I saw was that the mindset I attribute to my success as an entrepreneur—working as hard as possible to resolve issues and moving forward by accomplishing whatever tasks were necessary—was almost completely absent from government operations. This reflects an arrogant aspect of politics that can sometimes distract from our most important public policy debates with substantively absent rhetoric from politicians who elaborately point out obvious problems but never give specific solutions that can viably be implemented.

Only we shift government decision-making to reflect the intent of our policy goals can we get to the core of any issue by clearly defining our objectives and working to achieve observable progress. I ran to represent Hall and Forsyth counties in the state Senate because I felt that our government was predisposed to saying no to businesses without listening, with little regard for the consequences. Although I was outraged by the many government inefficiencies I discovered, in many cases, I found that the people who were administering government regulations had little or no incentive to accept anything other than a single method of compliance. Government must strike a balance, in which we shift our approach to implementing our stated goals by focusing on humanizing government operations to improve individual responsiveness and effectiveness. There is no area in which a "one-size-fits-all" mentality and mandate-based approach is more damaging to our ability to realize our potential than in public education.

When I decided to run for election to the state Senate I didn't have a background in politics, but I knew one thing for certain, we were hurting small business owners across the state of Georgia because of a failure to modernize the functions of government. As the stage became set for a historic Republican wave in the 1994 election cycle, I noticed more and more attention coalescing around my campaign platform. I wanted to make essential functions of government more efficient and to support the private sector whenever possible by eliminating purposeless directives. More than anything, I wanted to bring a common sense approach to government by solving public policy issues in a way that would allow regular people, who follow the rules, to be successful.

Although I started my 1994 Senate campaign without a network of political connections, I was fully committed to working as hard as possible to reach voters in Hall County and to build coalitions around the principles of opportunity and competent decision-making. When I started campaigning, if I encountered voters who were skeptical about my chances it was often for one of two reasons. First of all, if I were successful in the election, I would be the youngest member of Georgia's state Senate. I was twenty-eight years old, and some people assumed that my campaign was nothing more than a "trial run" to see if I might have a realistic chance of winning in 1996 or 1998. Even more frequently, I faced the challenge of transcending party identification to ask people who had never voted for anyone who wasn't a Democrat—but who I knew shared my values—to elect a Republican as their senator in Georgia's Capitol.

I will never forget one of the first conversations that I had after deciding to run for Senate. I went to visit my grandfather on my mother's side, Bill Miller, whom I called Papa Bill. We sat down in the living room at his house, and I said, "Papa Bill, I've got some good and some bad news to tell you." He seemed concerned—probably because of my own mix of excitement and anxiousness. After he asked what I had on my mind, I told him the good news first: Nita and I had talked it over, and I would be running for a seat in the state Senate. His eyes lit up, and he told me how proud he was that I was getting involved in public service. He started strategizing out loud—about how he could help, the people he was going to call on my behalf. Then he paused for a moment, remembering what I said earlier. He asked slowly: "Well, what's the bad news?"

Knowing that he had been a lifelong Democrat like many people in Gainesville and almost everywhere else in Georgia, I leaned in and told him I would be running as a Republican. Genuinely, he looked me directly in the eyes and didn't say anything. After pausing, he finally said: "I've never voted for a Republican before." My grandfather passed away many years ago, and to this day I still don't know if he voted for me or not. He did agree to let me put a sign up in his yard, though, and I suspect that he had something to do with the influx of signs that appeared around his neighbors' yards after I launched my campaign. This experience and similar encounters throughout my 1994 campaign helped me learn the lesson that I still value most in politics: Ultimately, people are, and should be, less concerned with party identification and more interested in effective governance and an individual's capacity for capable and ethical leadership.

I had a very difficult time raising money after I decided to launch my campaign. Being a Gainesville native and living in the poultry capital of the world, I had a lot of friends from our local industry—and I was frequently offered donations in poultry. This allowed me to host what I call chickencues (barbecued chicken dinners) each weekend, where I raised money for my campaign by selling tickets for $5. I also gained the opportunity to get my message out to a lot of voters. Almost exclusively through these events, I raised about $25,000 during my campaign.[13] Although that was a fraction of the amount spent by my opponent, and against all perceived odds, I won my first election. On November 4, 1994, I received 56 percent of the vote.[14]

Politics has a way of changing people. After I won my first election, I quickly became aware of how important it would be to guard against the temptation of getting caught up in my own political power. Commuting to Atlanta from Gainesville to spend time with Nita and our boys has helped me stay connected to what is most important in my life. I still recognize that the commitment I made in 1994 to return home to Gainesville at night was as much for myself as for our family. I grew up without a dad, and I always wanted to be the father to my three boys that I never had. Through the years, I have made every effort possible to be active in my boys' lives, coaching them, helping with homework, and guiding them through their own challenges as best as I can. Jared, Grant, and Carter have turned out to be fine young men. I remain grounded in reality enough to admit that this is not because of me but because of the love and support Nita extends to our entire family.

Shortly into my first session in the Senate, as I was still adjusting to my role and trying to find ways to make a difference, I had an experience that made me realize it would be a mistake to think too far outside of what mattered most to my district. It was late at night, and I received a call at home from a woman in Gainesville. She told me that she was concerned about a pesticide her neighbor had been spraying, which she said was making her cat sick. Then she started pleading for me to help protect her cat. There was a moment during that call when I thought to myself— after this difficult campaign I had just put my family through to be elected as a state senator, and still thinking about how I was going to help move the state of Georgia forward—*is it really my job to address this?* But I snapped back after the genuine concern in her voice got through to me. I recognized then that what one of my constituents was trying to get me to pay attention to was the most important thing to her life at that moment. And if it was that important to her, it should be that important to me because I was elected to be her representative.

Public service is about helping the constituents who we represent and making government work for people. Too often, we get caught up in trying to find the most creative-sounding idea in politics or the parts of a plan that perform the best in a poll. This causes us to become distracted from working together to find the best solutions. What I realized during my conversation with a constituent that night was that as an elected official, the most significant way I could make a difference was by serving my constituents as effectively as possible and working to make every aspect of our state government honest and accountable. In addition to electing representatives who make decisions on our behalf, we should also expect that in times of need we would be able to ask for help to find solutions to problems out of our control. I remember that conversation as a moment of clarity, which helped to shape how I view my role as a statewide policymaker.

The majority of my service in the Senate was as a member of the minority Republican caucus. It was not until 2003 that Republicans achieved a majority of seats in the Senate.[15] Before I became Chairman of the Finance Committee, which sets tax policy for the state of Georgia, I learned that I had to work to develop relationships with Democrats and Republicans to be an effective senator. I was able to pass meaningful legislation to benefit both my district and the state. But I felt called to do more. Following five terms of service in the state Senate, and a productive session as Chairman of the Senate Finance Committee, I realized that a more effective way to advance my vision for Georgia would be to become as a statewide policymaker. To build support for the comprehensive initiatives that I knew Georgia needed, I would have to engage citizens across our state. I wanted to offer people the ability to take greater ownership over their communities, and I needed their support just as much as I needed them to vote for me.

After receiving encouragement from leaders I respected, talking it over with my family and praying about it, I decided to run for lieutenant governor in 2006. If it was not a tough enough challenge to win a statewide election as a Republican, my opponent in the primary election was the nationally recognized Ralph Reed. He was the founding executive director of the Christian Coalition, and if elected, he clearly planned to use the Office of the Lieutenant Governor as a national platform. By June 2006, Reed had raised $2.5 million.[16] I, on the other hand, was a sitting state senator and was legally prohibited from raising any money until mid-April, and anyway, my legislative duties made it impossible to actively campaign until the General Assembly adjourned from session. Reporters pushed Reed to articulate his policy views further and further, and it became clear that many of his proposals either weren't specific to Georgia or didn't add up to much substance.

Even as an experienced legislator, I was sometimes taken aback by how much attention the media gave to the optics of the race and how little coverage was given to the issues that Georgia's voters cared about. I remember being approached by a reporter after speaking at a small event in LaGrange. When I asked which newspaper he was with, he casually replied with three words: "*Rolling Stone* magazine." I could not believe *Rolling Stone* was covering my campaign for lieutenant governor. And just one week later, I was speaking to guests after a campaign event when a reporter approached me to say he was from *GQ* magazine and wanted to ask a few questions.

Ralph Reed had been famously pictured on the cover of *Time* magazine. Maybe I would get to be on the cover of *Rolling Stone* or *GQ*, I thought. But after I read the articles that were written, in which it seemed both my candidacy and the issues facing Georgia's voters were presented as little more than footnotes in Ralph Reed's biography, I took notice that the coverage wasn't about us, it was about him. I was never on the cover of *Rolling Stone* or *GQ*, but I was profiled in both the *Tifton Gazette* and the *Gainesville Times*.[17] As it turned out, those were the articles that mattered on election day.

Despite the narrative characterized by the media, the 2006 election was very much about Georgia's future and much less so about which candidate had a bigger political press operation. I was committed to taking on an intensive campaign schedule so I could travel across our state, listening to concerns from people in as many of Georgia's communities as possible. At every stop, I related my vision for a renewed focus on how Georgia could become successful in our future. And on July 18, 2006, Republican voters overwhelmingly nominated me to run against Jim Martin in the general election. I maintained my focus on the same platform of working to expand opportunity, choice, and economic development so that we could focus our state government's operations on empowering more of our residents to become self-sufficient. I was successful, and voters elected me as the first—and only—Republican lieutenant governor in Georgia's history.

3

Educating Georgia
Our Past, Progress, and Future

History is a relentless master.
It has no present, only the past rushing into the future.
To try to hold fast is to be swept aside.[18]

—John F. Kennedy

There is no other state in possession of the same qualities that have made Georgia great, and which continue to position us for extraordinary growth in our future. The diversity of residents in urban, rural, and now widely suburban areas; the strength of our economy from the port of Savannah to expansive Metro-Atlanta and the manufacturing corridors of Middle and North Georgia; and the HOPE scholarship, which has helped to elevate our colleges and universities among the strongest institutions in the country, all provide exceptional value that must be incorporated into education reform.

We can't change the destination of our public school students overnight, but we can offer them a new direction. In this chapter, I will present a description of the development of our public education system. I will share experiences from the time that I was sworn into the state Senate until my election as lieutenant governor in 2006, and offer my perspective after three terms of service as a statewide official to explain the efforts to reform our education system. As we look for success in our future, it is critical that we understand Georgia's past progress, what we have learned from successful initiatives and, as enrollment in public schools approaches nearly two million students, how we can move past the formidable challenge of improving our education system to focus on individual achievement.

HOW DID WE GET HERE?

I served in the Senate under Governor Zell Miller, and I am proud that his legacy in education continues to make Georgia a better place to live. I have worked closely with both Governors Sonny Perdue and Nathan Deal to advance major reforms that I know have helped modernize our system of education and have allowed students to achieve better outcomes. In this section, I will discuss several of the legislative milestones that have contributed to the current dynamic of governance in Georgia's schools. I will also explain how, after being elected to represent Hall and Forsyth counties in the state Senate on a platform of making government more accountable and accessible to our citizens, I quickly became engaged in improving public education.

Article VIII of Georgia's Constitution directly sets the broad structure under which our statewide public education system operates.[19] Management and administrative authority are divided into powers and duties assigned by statute to an elected state superintendent of schools, the State Board of Education, local boards of education, and superintendents. Georgia's state superintendent is elected by voters and primarily acts as the CEO of the Department of Education, managing the more than seven hundred employees who encompass its extensive administrative network.[20]

The State Board of Education sets the tone for system-wide policy by approving curricula benchmarks, granting waiver requests, and enforcing district compliance with state and federal law. The board itself is made up of fourteen voting members, appointed from each congressional district by our governor. All 159 counties in Georgia and several cities, including Gainesville, Marietta, and Decatur, have an independent school board. Each board of education is responsible for staffing, budgeting, and implementing a management structure for the school systems under its jurisdiction.

In 1867, the first federal Department of Education was created to mimic European countries in gathering education statistics.[21] But quickly, the DOE was inserted into the post-bellum education policy of states. Between 1866 and 1939, when the Department of Education was merged into the Federal Security Agency, its role continued to expand.[22] From its reorganization into the Health, Education, and Welfare (HEW) agency in 1953, until the first federal education funding bill—the Elementary and Secondary Education Act of 1965 (ESEA) passed as one of the major War on Poverty programs—the DOE's reach into education policy slowly grew across different states.[23] Then, Georgia's own President Jimmy Carter created the modern federal Department of Education in 1979.[24]

Prior to 1965, education was almost entirely a local issue, and there were few central mandates that compare to our current balance of federal and state regulations. The No Child Left Behind Act of 2001 (known as NCLB) was passed as a reauthorization of the ESEA. Although it was re-named, the bill included a renewal of the Title programs, which impose requirements on states as conditions for accepting federal education funds. In terms of the federal government's approach in Georgia, NCLB is the most directly applicable program through which our difficulties in public education can be understood. Passed with bipartisan support, NCLB was supposed to be a standards-based education reform to set high academic standards and establish measurable goals as a way to improve individual outcomes for students.[25]

NCLB required states to develop assessments in math and reading as a requirement to keep receiving federal education funding. Each state was also required to set its own achievement standards for math and reading. Through the 2000s, the federal role in public education expanded—with an increased emphasis on annual testing, scoring academic progress, report cards, and teacher qualifications—and significant changes were made in the funding formula to reflect these new areas of emphasis.

I understand why President Bush saw an opportunity to make the nation stronger with No Child Left Behind. It did benefit Georgia to expose our weaknesses and the corresponding need for greater accountability in our education system. However, for Georgia, the program's effectiveness has run its course. High-stakes testing is the definition of a one-size-fits-all system. NCLB was a meaningful federal policy reform because it was an ambitious attempt to increase accountability. In 2012, Georgia was granted a waiver from following the No Child Left Behind law. One of the most important questions that we have to ask today is: *How can we define achievement in ways that most accurately apply to both teachers and students?*

The problem reflected by the measure of accountability used in No Child Left Behind is that, ironically, given the NCLB emphasis on closing subgroup achievement gaps, the performance of individual students has not been given much emphasis. Instead, statistics from standardized tests have been analyzed using comparisons—by class, grade, or most frequently, and with the highest stakes, using averages from entire schools and school systems. When we reduce our objectives to an average, by default, we are accepting the paradigm that in return for reaching a mean level of comprehension in the set educational benchmarks required at each grade level—in math, reading, or critical thinking—we are willing to accept that some students are going to fall through the cracks along the way for the sake of everyone else meeting the average and moving on. This is unacceptable.

The most basic problem with relying on high-stakes stand-ardized testing is the fact that, even with the best outcomes, nothing material can be promised to give value to the education our students are receiving. If standardized tests don't correlate to what students need to learn—which sometimes isn't possible—it's easy to imagine that even the most patient teachers will become frustrated. Over the past decade, members of both parties have voiced agreement that there are better ways for our schools to operate, and it's time for us to institute change.

In elementary and middle school, standardized tests can be used to evaluate fundamentally basic skills in core subjects. But outside of an essential foundation in math, reading, and writing, we do both students and teachers a disservice by not incorporating more direct formative evaluation methods into our primary schools as a way to determine academic success. If a student needs more time to learn the concepts required to advance on to new material, or conversely if a gifted student excels and is not being challenged, we should not cause both students to suffer by combining their scores so that we can claim them as part of an average school system.

Though I do recognize that testing provides a set of data necessary to evaluate basic subject knowledge and comprehension, and therefore will likely always be a part of the broader criterion used to evaluate student performance, we must provide greater flexibility by recognizing a range of methods to evaluate performance and account for the differences that naturally exist between individuals.

In 2015, Congress overwhelmingly passed the most recent reauthorization of ESEA to replace No Child Left Behind, renamed as the Every Student Succeeds Act (ESSA). In large part, ESSA is a recognition that the federal government's role in public education must be reduced in favor of restoring state and local control to more effectively enact reforms. ESSA is a step in the right direction, reducing the classroom role of standardized testing and promoting greater freedom and flexibility for decision makers.

Many innovative minds in education have started exploring how formative assessments can be implemented to better serve the functions of the high-stakes standardized tests that we currently use to evaluate student performance. This work must continue, and we have to increase the authority granted to our schools to implement formative assessments statewide.

Assessments, objectives for learning, and instructional strategies have to be implemented as part of a holistically designed strategic plan.[26]

• Learning objectives: What should students know after completing this course?

• Assessments: What tasks will determine if students are reaching the learning objectives required?

• Instructional strategies: Which lesson plans [in and out of class] will best align individual objectives before students are assessed?

Formative Assessment	*Summative Assessment*
The goal of formative assessment is to aggregate feedback that can be built upon by instructors and students to improve as they continue through the academic year. These serve as progress checks for students and instructors. Examples: • Students submit assignments that identify and discuss the purpose of each lecture. • Students complete outlines and rough drafts before submitting final papers. • Students submit written responses to class materials, then discuss these responses with classmates.	The role of summative assessment is to test proficiency after students complete each unit or course by measuring their achievement against an established standard. The outcome of a summative assessment can be used formatively if the results are used to build upon each individual's progress, ensuring that no student falls through the cracks. Examples: • Final exams. • Critiquing end of the year presentations. • Evaluations of faculty.

When Governor Joe Frank Harris began campaigning across the state for the Quality Basic Education Act, there was a widespread need to implement a consistent funding formula to create statewide parity in Georgia's schools irrespective of demographics or poverty levels. In 1985, Harris was successful in passing the Quality Basic Education funding formula into law. While there have been adjustments in the thirty years since, some of which I led during my service in the Senate, the underlying funding structure of our statewide public education system has largely remained intact. The QBE formula takes into consideration that each school system has a different tax base, a variable number of students, demand for different programs, and other factors that must be considered to fairly appropriate funding. The Quality Basic Education Act also established full-day kindergarten, formalized the authorization of the programs that initially comprised middle school, and prioritized an increase in funding for elementary school programs.

The enduring use of the QBE funding formula offers a standpoint through which our progress in improving Georgia's education system can be analyzed. On one hand, QBE markedly improved statewide education by offering countless students access to better programming, especially in rural areas and communities with high poverty rates. The majority of modifications to the QBE formula have been directed toward mandating specific uses for a portion of the funding that is allocated to school systems. Unlike many other issues that have become consumed by partisanship, Georgia's commitment to appropriating the majority of our state's public funds to education has contributed to a longstanding tradition of near unanimous approval of our annual budget. Alternatively—from the General Assembly's unanimous passage of the Quality Basic Education Act in 1985 to the longstanding use of the core QBE funding formula in today's school systems—this fundamentally important component of our system demonstrates how difficult it is to achieve change in public education. Many governors have tried and failed to change QBE in an effort to accomplish their respective goals in public education.

I do not believe that our greatest challenge in improving our public education system is merely a matter of adjusting overall funding or configuring a new formula to give more money to schools to implement new programs. Rather, our most significant obstacle is to reform our status quo operations by questioning how we think about public education in Georgia and returning as much authority as possible back to school districts so they can allocate more funding back to individual schools, giving them flexibility to use those funds to serve the needs of individual students.

The state of Georgia spends in excess of $10 billion per year on public education.[27] We should continue to reform the structure of the QBE formula to make sure that we are allocating funding to our school districts in a way that ensures every student has the opportunity to obtain a world-class education. If we were to simply give each district its fair share and total freedom to spend the money as its teachers, principals, and faculty members see fit to educate our children, the creativity and energy that would be released is unfathomable.

Zell Miller served as Georgia's lieutenant governor for sixteen years, from 1975 to 1991, and as governor for two terms, from 1991 to 1999. He rightfully holds a place in Georgia's history as one of our most effective leaders. Miller took office at a time when Georgia was nationally infamous for registering systemically poor scores in almost every comparative measurement of educational performance. For example, SAT scores in Georgia ranked among the lowest nationally, more than 100,000 residents aged twenty-five and older did not have more than a fifth grade education, and we had one of the largest per capita populations of students living in poverty.[28] By advancing the HOPE Scholarship and expanding Georgia's pre-kindergarten program, Miller was successful at both ends of the spectrum in providing our students with new opportunities to reach their potential.

The HOPE Scholarship has been transformational for Georgia. Not only because it has put college within reach for hundreds of thousands of students who would have never been able to afford tuition without it, but also because it has appreciably elevated the entire University System of Georgia. Before HOPE, the majority of our best students left Georgia to attend better universities out of state. Today, the opposite is true, and the majority of our state's best students now contribute to the notable strength of our own colleges and universities.[29] The number of students who are excelling academically and advancing to post-secondary success has also increased dramatically. By giving students the opportunity to achieve excellence with hard work and to take ownership over their learning, we took a huge step forward leading us to reach greater heights in the twenty-first century.

As a parent, I initially recognized several of the issues that I would later offer legislative solutions to fix because I observed how our education system functioned in relation to my own children's performance. Drawing on my childhood, in which I constantly moved around and attended eight different elementary schools before I reached sixth grade, I wanted my boys to have the stability that I didn't have. Nita and I sought out public schools in Hall County that we thought would best meet our family's needs. Initially, we were able to send our two oldest boys to schools that impressed us with effective leadership from good principals. But when our county implemented a mandatory attendance zone, our youngest son was restricted from the public school choice that we had previously been offered. As time went on, things got worse. It started to feel like we were being shut out of participating in our son's education. Oftentimes when my wife and I tried to contribute specific input and become more actively engaged, our voices went unheard.

After one of our youngest son's completed the third grade, Nita and I received his standardized test scores and found out that he was deficient in reading comprehension. With no information outside of his standardized test results to guide us, we requested a meeting with his teacher. When we asked about our son's performance, we were told not to worry: he would catch up on his own in the fourth grade, and there would be no focused effort to get him up to grade level in reading.

Reading comprehension is the core component that allows students to access the incredible volume of knowledge available in our schools, libraries, and across every dimension of life. It seemed like our son's need for help in grasping the skills necessary to learn was being dismissed by the school and ignored by the system. We took matters into our own hands and enrolled him in a Sylvan Learning Center program specifically designed to get him up to grade level in reading. After he completed his individualized course that summer, our son registered at a sixth-grade reading level. Fortunately our family could afford to get outside help to prevent our son from falling behind, but I grew increasingly concerned with the lack of accountability for individual student performance in our education system.

Georgia's dropout rate remained persistently high, and I became aware that a staggering number of students were being promoted to the next grade level without regard for the fact they had not caught up with their peers, like our system assumed they would, but continued to fall further behind. These students were being sent down a path that, for many, would lead them to eventually disengage and drop out of high school, only to enter a job market in which they would face the unlikely prospect of finding employment that could viably support a family. One of the most common reasons that students drop out of high school is because they fail to see relevance in the material they are learning.[30] Once students fall behind, if they are unable to envision how their education will impact their lives in a positive way, it becomes extremely difficult for them to get caught up academically.

One of my early efforts to reform education in the Senate was a proposal that I authored on public-school choice, inspired by my son's negative experience with mandatory attendance zones.[31] The bill that I wrote didn't mandate that every district in Georgia offer parents the right to choose which public school their children would attend. Instead, I took an approach that I have found to be much more effective in encouraging schools to adopt programs that increase choice or opportunity. Under my proposal, we would have given schools an incentive to fill extra space available by allowing students from within that school's county to apply for those spots. Ultimately, individual communities would have retained the ability to make a decision for themselves on public school choice, allowing the policy's effectiveness to rise or fall based on merit and local input. I did not anticipate the level of opposition that would be waged by the educational establishment against my bill, and my proposal failed.

Notwithstanding that my first attempt at introducing what I thought was a commonsense reform was unsuccessful, I felt an even greater responsibility to improve our system by taking on what I saw as a much more systemic problem in public education.

My focus turned to ending the fundamentally flawed practice of social promotion in our state, which put pressure on schools and teachers to continue promoting students to the next grade level, regardless of their performance or ability. Working from my own experience with my son's difficulty in reading comprehension, I started to look further into Georgia's graduation rates and made a connection. After a long process studying this issue, I authored a bill with Eric Johnson, Tom Price, and Sonny Perdue that would have required schools to social promotion in the third grade if students were unable to meet basic reading comprehension requirements.[32] Again, we faced much more opposition than I had initially imagined. Legislators were asking questions such as: *"If we require students to reach this level in reading comprehension, then aren't we going to have thirteen or fourteen year olds trapped in the third grade?"*

I couldn't believe that the educational establishment had become so direct in its arguments against performance-based achievement that its members were opposed to implementing even the most basic accountability safeguards to serve as checkpoints for students along the way in our public education system. Our proposal to end social promotion initially failed. Eventually, in 2001, we reached a compromise with the Democrat majority to end social promotion by specifically requiring the use of CRCT (Criterion-Referenced Competency Tests) test scores as the accountability mechanism for reaching an acceptable level of reading comprehension in the third grade.[33] We know today that centering the focus of our teachers on preparing students to score well on the CRCT is not nearly good enough for Georgia's students. We can enable teachers, principals, and supporting faculty to accept individual accountability for the students in every single one of our schools without being forced to rely on summative assessments of their performance that consider high-stakes standardized test scores alone.

When we discuss proposals for comprehensive public education reform, it can be very difficult to separate the basic structural foundation that allows our education system to function from factors that practically apply to managing schools, teachers, and how students are taught. Most recently, the Race to the Top section of the American Recovery and Reinvestment Act of 2009 required states to identify standards and assessments to prepare students for success in college and a career, to build systems that collect data on student growth, and to inform teachers and leadership teams about how to improve instruction.[34] Some of these reforms seem so basic in intent that it's challenging to understand why the government can't just mandate our schools to do better. The reason that we can't improve performance by demanding the results that everyone agrees we need to achieve from the top down is because we are not building an assembly line where we can drop a five-year-old off in August, and pick up an eighteen-year-old who is prepared for a post-secondary education thirteen years later.

Education, like it or not, is the collective result of the role that parents, teachers, and society play in influencing our children's development. As I discuss education policy milestones that have been enacted, both on issues that have been among my major policy priorities and in areas that I do not believe have been successful, I attempt to explain the real effect, as I see it, on our education system. Significant progress has been made over the past three decades; however, we continue to possess tremendous, unrealized potential in every division of our public-education system. It's critical to understand that our goal must be to provide each and every student enrolled in Georgia's public schools with a path towards graduating with a meaningful high-school degree and with a vision to succeed in his or her future.

The best way to accomplish this objective is to offer flexibility and choices that allow our schools to function as independently as possible under effective local leaders, who agree to reach measurable outcomes outlined in an individualized plan of action. To achieve this shift, we do not need to request changes in federal policy or a new omnibus legislative effort from Georgia's General Assembly. We have already passed the Charter Systems Act and the District Accountability Act.

The Charter Systems Act [SB 39][35]

This 2007 law grants waivers for almost all state laws and state board rules in exchange for a district accepting academic targets and committing to implement local school governance.

The District Accountability Act [HB 1209][36]

This 2008 law granted specific waivers of state law and related state board rule in exchange for a district accepting school-level academic targets set by the Governor's Office of Student Achievement (GOSA) and consequences for failing to achieve those targets.

Reforming our public education system to renew the foundational promise of opportunity that we've made to our citizens will require us to change the culture of our public schools. Over the next several years, all of Georgia's stakeholders in education must unite to guide a transformation that will reward innovation and achievement. This will require a concentrated effort to engage parents, appropriately respect and compensate our teachers and principals, and establish a real line of communication between each of our schools and businesses, service organizations, post-secondary institutions, and the other valuable entities whose livelihoods depend on the strength of our public education system.

Ownership

Who Takes Ownership In Our Public Education System, And Why Does It Matter?

In the 2015–2016 school year, more than 1,750,000 students enrolled in Georgia's public schools.[37] As the father of three boys, I understand that all students learn at different paces, and different people approach learning in a variety of ways. Unfortunately, many school systems are unable to focus on improving individual student performance because they don't have the ability to freely allocate the funding they receive for each student enrolled in their schools. There are two potential public policy approaches that Georgia can take to improve our public schools. We can follow the model set by countless former governors to impose statewide mandates on all of Georgia's school systems. But, as proven by many other mandates, we will likely only hurt students by increasing pressure on teachers for compliance. Or we can pursue the method that I have advocated, in which we comprehensively reevaluate public education and approach our objectives system-by-system in each school's community.

Public education has always been, and will always be, the highest priority of our state's government. After I was elected lieutenant governor in 2006, still mindful of my experience with education in the budget process as a member of the Senate Appropriations Committee, I spent several months working to determine how I could meaningfully reform education. I studied the problems in school systems across the state, systems that range in size from several hundred students to more than 160,000. I evaluated the consequences of failure for students, and I analyzed how limitations in our current system can reduce the number of opportunities available to many students in Georgia.

Based on my research, I reached the conclusion that our students will never be able to rise to their full potential academically or professionally unless we move away from a top-down approach. Our education system must be based on achievement and promoting academic ability, entrepreneurship, and technical-skill training. Strengthening our schools requires us to rethink the role shared by the state of Georgia, principals, teachers, parents, and community institutions in public education.

When ownership is attached to a culture of participation in all of our schools, and everyone plays a role in the education of our students, the results are extraordinarily positive. Teachers have the most important responsibilities because they provide creative and effective ways to instruct students on a daily basis, regularly working long hours outside the classroom. Principals and instruction specialists are the leaders who help teachers do their jobs. They visit classrooms daily to observe teaching, as well as co-teach, model, and coach our teachers. In highly effective schools, everyone is involved, from custodians and cafeteria staff who drill students on basic math and literacy skills as they walk through the halls or eat lunch, to bus drivers who ensure their riders are picked up on time and have a safe trip to school. The school's entire staff ensures that the school's climate makes students feel safe and cared for, and that students are challenged to learn at all times. Parents, of course, play an important role by ensuring their children come to school ready to learn after a good night's sleep and have support to get their homework done.

We must do everything possible to foster an environment of innovation in our public schools. No two students learn in the same way, and no two communities in Georgia have the same resources. Each school must have the freedom to implement new ideas and programs designed to better engage students and improve academic performance. And in communities that are interested in forming partnerships, we should encourage school systems to support cooperative arrangements with businesses or educationally focused organizations.

When we have an education system that can effectively meet the needs of each student and provide the necessary foundation for all students to be professionally successful, we will experience lasting economic growth. To reach this objective, each school's leadership must adopt a collaborative approach in which they work with teachers and faculty to incorporate all available resources to better prepare students for their futures. Success is based on an individual's personal experiences and can be defined in many ways; however, if our public education system doesn't provide students with an opportunity to challenge themselves and explore their academic and professional interests as they prepare for post-secondary education or a career after graduation, then our system is failing us.

My first legislative effort to reform education as Georgia's lieutenant governor was to allow school systems to adopt a new governance model called a charter system under which their students would be able to attend kindergarten through twelfth grade.[38] This was the first program of its kind in the nation, and we have recorded overwhelmingly positive results since the Charter Systems Act was signed into law in 2007. The structure of the charter systems model for schools was inspired by my career in banking and the system that I worked under as chairman of the board of directors for Southern Heritage Bank.

By providing an opportunity for school systems to submit an application to become a charter system, I wanted to let individual systems demonstrate with a strategic plan they would be able to govern themselves more effectively than could a top-down government agency. I also recognized that all of our public education institutions have to break down their silos and work together. Communication between primary and secondary school leaders is essential to maintaining an inclusive education system and ful-filling our mission of educating all of Georgia's children. Charter systems are the schools with the greatest degree of freedom and flexibility because of the higher accountability standards they have committed to following. As a result, they have consistently pro-duced innovative programs and targeted pathways to reward and develop student achievement. Although I recognize that not every school in Georgia will perform best as part of a charter system, I have no doubt that there are countless programs that will be devel-oped in charter systems that could benefit students under different models of governance.

In a charter system, the process of reform begins by establish-ing a direct line of accountability with a contract between the school system and the state of Georgia. The purpose of an ac-countability contract is to outline expectations under a five-year strategic plan, establish metrics for success, and give the school system the ability to exercise school-level management. As long as schools are in compliance with an overarching set of agreed upon educational benchmarks, they are free to allocate their annual budgets as they see fit, whether to add instructional materials, in-crease teacher pay, or realign course content and schedules. This is a critical part of reform, which allows each school to address indi-vidual problems that have historically prevented some students from receiving an adequate education.

After we prepare students for academic success in elementary and middle school, it is critical to allow them to grow within our system by taking advantage of all four years of high school. Estab-lishing College and Career Academies was my second major legis-lative effort as lieutenant governor.[39] This reform was targeted at giving high schools and communities a path to allow their students to enroll in a technical certification program or advanced courses that count towards the credit hours required to graduate from a four-year college.

Georgia's College and Career Academies are helping us excel beyond other states in expanding our capacity to provide students with the ability to graduate from high school with an associate degree or technical certification. I have made it one of my highest priorities to give every high school student in Georgia access to a College and Career Academy by 2020. We must give value to the degrees that our graduates earn by allowing them to develop marketable skills, to gain work experience through internships, or to advance their transition into a post-secondary education. It is critically important that by the time students graduate from eighth grade, they are proficient at grade level, or beyond, in reading, writing, mathematics, science, and social studies.

I believe that most people in Georgia want our state to offer an accessible education to every student that allows them to pursue any career path they choose. In the following chapters, I will present my vision for public education in Georgia in detail and offer an analysis of our system and the challenges that we face. After I define success in public education, I will explain the pathways for improvement that should be available for every school system. By discussing models of innovation, opportunities to provide students with more academic choices, and ways to expand community collaboration as we move forward, I will demonstrate how we can give every student in Georgia the opportunity to reach his or her full potential.

4

What Do We Value?
All Teachers Must Be Exceptional

A teacher affects eternity; he can never tell where his influence stops.[40]

—Henry Adams

I think that everyone wants the ability to make life better: for themselves, for their kids, and for their communities. Each of us wants to leave something behind when we're gone. We want our kids to have more opportunity than we had, in part because the idea of leaving a legacy to improve the lives of others is ingrained in the fabric of American society. The act of service is found in all walks of life, just as there is dignity in accepting any honest job. It will take a concentrated effort to restore the respect that every individual in our workforce deserves, and to make sure that all people have the opportunity to earn a successful future.

With respect to the outcome for individual students, what is the purpose of public education? A large part of this book is devoted to answering this question and to defining how we can reach our goal of giving every student a path to success. It's indisputable that our most valuable assets in our public schools are the teachers. We must change the way in which Georgia views teachers in order to allow our 122,000 educators to utilize their true potential in classrooms.

Teachers are public servants. In any given classroom scenario, teachers are the ones most directly tasked with evaluating the level of comprehension with which students enter class and then ensuring that each student learns the subject matter to the best of his or her ability. At a minimum, teachers are required to write and present daily lesson plans, grade assignments, and maintain a constructive learning environment free of disruptions. This is not to mention the large amounts of paperwork that many teachers are required to submit, depending on their discipline and specific position.

But the one aspect of a public school teacher's job description, which distinctly makes so many of the educators across our state such remarkable public servants, is the fact that teachers dedicate an extraordinary amount of time and effort to their students. I didn't get into politics to make money, and teachers don't go into their profession pursuing wealth. There is no one thing that will make a teacher perfect, just as there is no single definition of success. But despite the fact that the countless hours that teachers work are rarely recorded on a timesheet, it is incredibly impactful when teachers invest their time to help students become successful.

A teacher's basic responsibilities to students far surpass the call to service that even the most selfless people feel. I cannot imagine the frustration that teachers in school systems across our state feel when they are unable to get through and make a difference to those students who they know are struggling because of the antiquated structure of our public schools. In place of policies that make sense for our children's futures, we have demanded status quo compliance from schools for the sake of maintaining a one-size-fits-all system that mandates that the majority of our schools meet an arbitrary academic average. When we establish school-level governance in all of Georgia's public schools, the most fundamental changes that students and parents will experience will be addressed using the newfound freedom and flexibility given to our teachers. Correspondingly, schools will finally be able to acknowledge the work that individual teachers do—and appropriately compensate them above and beyond the state salary schedule.

I am committed to making sure through all of our implemented reforms, that we protect the promises made to current and retired teachers and work to do everything possible to attract more educators.

In addition to recognizing the aptitude of every student, teachers have to match the way in which each student learns with the knowledge and skills they need to acquire. Flexibility is essential for any organization that serves human beings, but it is difficult to overstate the damage that we can inflict upon students when we strictly limit the decision-making authority given to teachers. The people who are best prepared to solve problems in our public education system are teachers, which is obvious to most observers. Unfortunately, many teachers face resistance from supervisors when they attempt to teach using innovative lesson plans. We must trust our teachers to perform to the best of their abilities, and we should do everything possible to give them the support necessary to go above and beyond as they educate their students.

To be successful—at a minimum—we must value teachers enough to humanize education by empowering them with every available resource, including decision-making authority, to better educate students in their classrooms. The only way to give principals and teachers ownership to make decisions over what's best for their students is with school-level management. Imagine approaching anyone who works in a county school system office and asking: *What are our overall objectives for all 1.7 million students in our public education system?*[41] *How do we all measure success? And who gets to make the important decisions?* The structure of our current system makes it far too difficult to provide answers to these questions.

From Atlanta to Savannah, Valdosta to Rome, and in every city in between, our schools reflect the unparalleled level of diversity that gives our state so much strength. Each of our schools should be given the flexibility to address the unique challenges they face, and the structure of our public education system should reflect the needs of the individual students within all 2,300 public schools in Georgia.[42] After teachers are given decision-making authority and schools adopt local management structures, educators must assume a contributing role, along with principals and members of each school's leadership, in directing the operational structure of their schools.

If we hope to systematically integrate prominent industries and academically valuable organizations into our statewide educational network, we must first allow teachers to match their school's resources with the needs of their students. Nothing presents a greater challenge to both students and teachers than when students are put into classes they are unprepared for, as they are—barring some extraordinary academic intervention—set up to fail.

One of the most prominent debates on how to improve student academic performance over the past decade has focused on the issue of mandatory class sizes and whether or not to implement a cap on the number of students per teacher. I don't believe there is evidence to support the idea that a cap based on a student-to-teacher ratio is something that every school should be mandated to uniformly maintain. The fact that many groups would argue that class size mandates could be used to achieve a given academic average is the ultimate example of finding a lazy and expensive solution to address one of the symptoms of the larger challenge that we face in public education. It doesn't take a Stanford economist to make the commonsense determination that, "The effectiveness of the teacher in the classroom is far, far more important than how many students are in the classroom."[43] Still, Eric Hanushek, senior fellow at the Hoover Institution of Stanford University, has conducted research that empirically supports this conclusion.

An analysis of the logic behind designating a general cap of students to each teacher relies on the implication that if we divide the amount of resources and individual attention each student requires—hypothetically—in elementary school, a 17-student-to-1-teacher ratio results in a successful average outcome. This is not to say that an average of 17 students in all of the classes offered, with corresponding maximum and minimum enrollment parameters, as it might make sense to use, would be acceptable. Rather, it's almost always ruled easier to mandate an all-or-nothing policy. This is just one example of how debates in education policy have devolved into what sometimes seem like an effort to enact deliberately ineffectual mandates that will result in the majority of schools opting out and applying for a waiver.

A 2013 report conducted by Education Resource Strategies in partnership with the Georgia Department of Education set out to evaluate our state's use of resources to determine recommendations for how our schools can strategically shift to increase student achievement. Overall, the report and policy audit found that it is in Georgia's best interest—for the benefit our students—to continue moving away from policies that mandate specific uses of resources, shifting to policies that grant flexibility to school-level leaders who accept greater accountability around improving outcomes for students. In particular, the report notes: "having class size mandates in place at all presupposes a one-teacher paradigm that too often generates one-size-fits-all classroom staffing practices, deterring districts from leveraging class size flexibilities to implement innovative classroom models."[44]

Providing schools with increased freedom doesn't mean that we need to abandon all order or reason. In reality, the concept of school level governance is founded on establishing latitude for schools to operate by setting reasonable boundaries within an accountability contract. Giving individual school systems authority to allocate their own budgets, which are already appropriated based on the number of students enrolled, not only allows us to more equitably determine the number of students that should be in each classroom, but also to match instructional resources with those students' needs. The leaders of each school are also able to more effectively measure the academic range of classes offered against the number of teachers and faculty employed against how much is spent on instructional materials—all in the context of a complete annual budget.

Although we will never be able to adequately compensate teachers for their contribution to society, we owe it to them to make our best effort. An essential part of treating teachers fairly is permitting individual school systems to reward teachers beyond the state minimum salary. Teachers receive a base salary determined by the state of Georgia, and local school boards have the ability to supplement that income. A teacher with a bachelor's degree will earn a base starting salary of approximately $33,000.[45] If teachers have advanced degrees, they will earn more within the same salary schedule. Every year for up to twenty years, teachers receive scheduled raises that do not consider performance.[46] On average, teachers make $53,000 a year, and in 2015, our state spent more than $6 billion to pay Georgia's 122,000 educators.[47]

The compensation system that we use for public school teachers doesn't exist anywhere in the private sector and presents a critical challenge to the success of our schools. Conceptually, Georgia's annual salary schedule is grounded in our budget-making process. It allows our state, and each school system, to project exactly how much we will pay teachers for decades to come. Our system has been efficient but not effective. *Can we really expect teachers to stay in their jobs forever?* It may sound like an exaggeration, but we do. Many of the problems occurring in our schools are arising because of quick fixes that we have attempted to implement statewide, on decades-long scales. These policies have always seemed easier, required less effort, and almost never spark any major criticism or controversy when they are renewed. However, there are limits to any projection, and our system of paying teachers is failing us.

Educators in Georgia enter their careers knowing they will not reach their full earning potential for twenty years. *Could anything be more uninspiring to young and ambitious professionals?* There are many people who are deterred from becoming public school teachers because of the incredible personal sacrifice that our state-mandated salary schedule demands. Employment data demonstrates that thousands of people leave the teaching profession within just a few years, seeking a career in the private sector where pay is connected to performance. Furthermore, our tenure-based structure makes it exceedingly difficult for people to become educators after working in another profession.

Every school should be able to offer teachers multiple earning opportunities beyond the state-mandated salary schedule. By making available specific choices—to teach a certain number of classes, mentor another teacher, sponsor an extracurricular or coach a sport—we will provide teachers with the incentive to do work that is necessary for our students to be successful. In return for working long hours and dedicating themselves to our children's learning, teachers should be compensated when they take on additional responsibilities.

Working as a public school teacher is more than just a job; it is a vocation and a calling. We have to give our teachers more respect as professionals, recognizing that master teachers who have three to five years of experience, and individuals who transition from other careers into teaching, can both contribute valuable experience that will enrich the quality of our schools. In addition to removing barriers that encourage some teachers to leave the profession, we should encourage people with a diverse range of career trajectories to become public school teachers so that each community's schools can accurately reflect the diversity in our economy and in our society. Teachers should be valued as individual leaders, participating in directing the structure of their school's operations along with principals, administrators, and supporting faculty members.

No One Achieves Success Alone

From kindergarten until they graduated from high school, my three boys attended school in Hall County. There is a six-year age difference between my oldest son, Jared, and my youngest son, Carter, so for more than nineteen years, Nita and I watched our community's public schools, where our boys were enrolled, grow alongside our family. Almost every day we invested time and energy into their educations: helping with homework, communicating with teachers, and encouraging our boys to challenge themselves academically. After graduating from Johnson High School in 2014, Carter now attends Georgia State University, the same university where Jared and Grant earned their degrees. Like all families do, our boys have had ups and downs, and they each navigated individual challenges in school, but their continued success gives me more pride than I have experienced from anything else in my life.

Nita and I worked hard to make sure that our children received the best education possible to prepare them for the future. In the process, we met a number of incredible teachers who made a tremendous impact on the way that our boys thought, and sparked their interest in learning about a variety of subjects.

I remember back to when I was growing up and didn't have much to fall back on; I struggled in school, and my path was uncertain, but I was blessed to have teachers who went out of their way to help me. I wouldn't be where I am today if it weren't for the exceptional public school teachers who believed in my potential.

When I started sixth grade at Jones Elementary—my first year at the eighth and final elementary school I attended—I had a teacher named Mrs. Barfield who put an extraordinary amount of effort into helping me learn. She saw that I had potential and a desire to do well but was being held back by academic deficiencies in different areas. At times, it might have seemed easier to let me give up and repeat the sixth grade. However, if that thought ever crossed Mrs. Barfield's mind, it didn't affect her unwavering determination to help me learn. Day in and day out, Mrs. Barfield invested her time to get me up to grade level. When I finally caught up, she challenged me to reach for higher levels.

No one achieves success alone. It is impossible to put a price tag on what teachers represent to their students, schools, and communities. Nothing will ever replace the contribution that our teachers make to society. Appropriately reflecting the importance of these roles is paramount to reaching any of the goals we set for our students. There are certain heroic people in history that everyone admires: presidents, innovators, Nobel Prize winners. We admire people who have accomplished something that inspires us to dream, but every day, teachers change the world.

There are many teachers I can vividly remember having an impact that changed my life. I remember Mr. Colson, my assistant principal at South Hall Middle School, who challenged me to grow and learn from my mistakes—which usually meant showing toughness I would later learn to appreciate. I will never forget Mrs. Deadwyler, my high school counselor who guided me towards enrolling in courses I might have otherwise avoided because of their difficulty, but which made me a more capable student. I will always be grateful to Mrs. Kesler and Mrs. Vaughan, who went above and beyond to ensure I developed a love of learning. These are just a few, among many, who I can say *with certainty* had a hand in helping me become the person I am today. While everyone who works contributes something to help our society collectively advance, teachers directly shape what our future will look like. We have to appropriately compensate and encourage growth in those talented individuals who dedicate their lives to teaching, mentoring, and guiding children to reach for, and achieve their dreams.

5

Freedom and Fairness for Georgia

A 'No' uttered from the deepest conviction is better than a 'Yes' merely uttered to please, or worse, to avoid trouble.[48]

—Mahatma Gandhi

My role as Georgia's lieutenant governor has permitted me to travel across our state, and whenever I give public remarks, I always try to incorporate time to answer questions from the audience or media outlets. Throughout my campaigns, and at any public event I host, answering specific questions on issues people care about provides the best forum to explain my policy views. I can point to innumerable experiences with people who have contributed to understanding of how to further our state's development and my ability to better represent our citizens. But I have also spent a lot of time reflecting on the answer to one question, which is critically important to communicate before we will be able to improve our education system. The central question that we should never stop asking is: *With respect to the outcome for individual students, what is the purpose of public education?*

The answer has far reaching implications that can incorporate any number of dimensions, and to a large degree, it is what orders our society and helps set most of the public's priorities. A high school diploma has to be more significant than a prerequisite to a four-year degree or an indication to employers that a job applicant has a minimal level of skills. Our public schools must provide every student with a foundation for his or her career. The question of the outcomes we expect can also be viewed very narrowly. We can analyze individual outcomes in the third grade or the impact of elective classes offered to students in middle school. Before we can establish metrics for success, we must adopt a new governance approach under which each school is allowed to determine, measure, and realize realistic benchmarks for its students' performance.

We have to understand how singular functions of our education system are organized within each school's structure of governance so that we can distinguish when a system's policies contribute to either the success or the failure of its students. I believe that the purpose of public education is to provide a system through which everyone and anyone can achieve academic, social, and professional excellence. For all of our students to have access to the education they deserve, we must focus our attention on helping every school empower students with the knowledge and skills necessary to become self-sufficient. We cannot accept anything less than for every student to be able to reach his or her own definition of success.

Too many people blame our teachers for poor academic performance in our schools and yet refuse to give them the flexibility required to educate our students. This is equivalent to blaming a football coach for losing games while preventing him from calling the plays. We have to recognize that parents, families, and communities play a fundamentally important role in each child's development. We cannot, however, use this point as an excuse to explain away the failure to provide some children with what is required for their well-being and growth as a person as they continue their education in our schools. We all have a role to serve when it comes to public education. There are countless parents, teachers, and residents in our state's counties who understand exactly what our education system is offering students and know that we can do better. Many of these individuals are waiting for the chance to contribute to a superior quality system.

Historically, almost everyone has acknowledged that the most persistent challenge our high schools have faced is unacceptably high dropout rates. We have to confront widespread disengagement from students who feel like what they are learning is not applicable to their lives. Restoring real marketable value to the diplomas our students are earning is imperative. To accomplish this objective, it's incumbent upon us to remove the top-down resistance directed towards many teachers when they attempt to design innovative lesson plans to offer new perspectives in instructing students.

In Georgia's future, there will continue to be an important role for our state superintendent and state board of education, just as there will be for local boards and superintendents. That role is to support each of Georgia's 2,300 schools. Ultimately, it is each school's mission to provide its students with access to teachers and resources that promote learning, reward academic engagement, facilitate achievement, and allow them to successively build a foundation for their futures when they advance from grade to grade.

Throughout my service in government, I have participated in our state's legislative debate over education policy. Several years ago, I reached the conclusion that the only way to resolve the majority of our problems in public education would be to internally develop solutions at each school. The problems we face in public education have not changed, but in recent years, our ability to implement transformational reform has gained substantial momentum because of advancements in technology that now allow us to measure, communicate, and verify student academic performance. The assets that every school has available should be utilized to empower teachers, principals, and local leaders to implement and operate a governance system better suited for the twenty-first century.

In 1994, as part of my platform to advance fair and effective state government, I campaigned to change the way that schools finance construction projects. School districts were using General Obligation Bonds to pay for capital construction and assessing each district's property owners at the tax rate needed to meet their annual bond obligations. My first legislative proposal as a state senator was a constitutional amendment to permit local boards of education to finance school construction by placing a referendum on the ballot and asking voters to approve a Special Local Option Sales Tax of 1 percent.[49] For the passage of my constitutional amendment, a two-thirds majority would be required in both chambers of the General Assembly. To become law, a majority of Georgia's voters would have to cast ballots in support of the amendment in the next general election.

Quickly, I encountered firm opposition from prominent lobbyists and leaders in different segments of the large and diverse network of education organizations. I had just been sworn into the state Senate and, naïvely, I didn't think it mattered that the Republican Party only held twenty-one of fifty-six seats.[50] Back then, many of my Democratic colleagues were not that far apart from Republicans ideologically, and Zell Miller had just started his second term as governor by presenting a notably conservative agenda. It wasn't relevant to my bill that I didn't have experience as a legislator because I had enough practical experience to understand that it didn't make sense for school districts to disproportionally force property owners alone to pay off new cycles of debt.

During the 1995 session, the chairman of the Senate Finance Committee was Terrell Starr. Senator Starr was a true statesman. He respected every senator and maintained a willingness to discuss any idea based on merit. After I submitted my bill and it was assigned to the finance committee, I asked to meet with Starr to talk about my constitutional amendment. As I sat down, he pulled my bill out of one of his desk drawers. I told him that I was planning to work as hard as possible to pass my legislation, and I asked if he had any advice or concerns. He responded by saying: "Well the first piece of advice that I will give you is—the next time you want a bill passed out of my committee, I suggest that you do not bring me a bill with only Republican signatures." I soon recognized that to get anything passed in the Senate, I would need support from legislators in both parties.

Starr went on to tell me that he supported the concept behind my constitutional amendment, and that he was going to help me to get it passed. I took Starr's advice and worked to rewrite a compromise with legislators who were in opposition to my bill that we could all support. The day after I finished drafting a new constitutional amendment, I discovered that the chairman of the Senate Education Committee had introduced a carbon copy of my bill.[51] He used virtually the same language and was attempting to rush his bill through his committee so that he could bring it to the Senate floor and pass it before my bill. I was outraged and almost in disbelief that one of my colleagues was so transparently attempting to take credit for my work.

I made an appointment to meet with Pierre Howard, who was then Georgia's lieutenant governor. The primary constitutional duty of our lieutenant governor is to serve as president of the Senate, acting as the chamber's presiding officer. I met with Howard and explained to him that another senator had re-introduced—and was attempting to pass—a duplicate of a legislative compromise that I had worked to develop. He agreed that it wasn't fair for another senator to claim my bill, and offered a compromise: "I'll tell you what we're going to do. We're going to have you and the chairman of the Education Committee co-author a new bill. That legislation will be what we pass in the Senate." I was a freshman Republican senator, and the Democratic lieutenant governor Pierre Howard was listening to me complain about the Democratic chairman of the Senate Education Committee. He didn't have to offer me anything. He could have easily told me that I needed to wait my turn to pass legislation. But the lieutenant governor wanted to do what was right. What Howard said in support of my ownership over the bill—even as a freshman Republican—is that he respected the voice of every single senator.

In November 1996, voters in Georgia approved a constitutional amendment to allow local boards of education to call a referendum on a SPLOST, or a 1 percent local sales tax that could be collected for up to five years to finance school construction. My first attempt to amend Georgia's Constitution was successful, and I gained valuable legislative experience, helping me serve as an effective state senator.[52]

I also learned one of the most valuable lessons that politics has taught me, and which, to this day, influences how I view my role as lieutenant governor. What Howard's actions taught me is that every senator is elected by voters in Georgia to represent their interests in the General Assembly. Whether a senator's constituents are Democrats or Republicans, everyone in Georgia deserves to have their voice represented by their elected officials.

This chapter is about creating a new governance structure for our public schools. Governing authority in our country is administered under the United States Constitution, which has been amended twenty-seven times since it was adopted in 1788.[53] The US Constitution doesn't mention education, whereas Georgia's Constitution includes the word education more than one hundred times. Article VIII of our Constitution is titled Education and establishes a network of state and local government offices to administer primary, secondary, and higher education. In chapter three, I provide background on the general structure of public education in Georgia.

Instead of outlining specific procedures for individual schools and systems to follow, Georgia's Constitution gives authority to the General Assembly, the governor, and to leaders in our education system to appropriately determine how to offer students the best possible education. This is in line with the origin and foundation of our state government described in Paragraph I, Section II of Georgia's Constitution. It states that: "All government, of right, originates with the people, is founded upon their will only, and is instituted solely for the good of the whole."[54]

Personally, I take pride in the US Constitution and consider it to be one of the most significant documents ever written, but without Georgia's Constitution, we could not effectively govern our state. Accountability contracts between each school district and the state of Georgia have a comparable effect in defining a framework for school-level authority through which principals, teachers, and communities can expressively take advantage of every available opportunity to improve. We have extraordinary academic programs and many capable leaders in schools throughout our state. But we aren't doing enough statewide to apply a cohesive method to determine who is responsible for which duties, or to set meaningful objectives for individual schools to pursue.

During the past four decades, although our state and federal governments have both dramatically increased their involvement in different aspects of our public education system, Georgia has never adopted an effective standard model of governance for our primary and secondary schools. In recent years, the majority of our public schools have essentially been asked to meet the status quo—to reach an average, find a common way of teaching, and to rely on high-stakes standardized testing to evaluate their students' performance.

Writing an accountability contract to enable school-level decision-making makes teachers more capable of promoting academic success to effectively use the resources that rightfully belong to each of their students. This leads to offering students more enrollment options earlier in their education, in elementary and middle schools, while making sure that every student masters the fundamentals of mathematics, science, social studies, reading, and writing before advancing to high school. Principals, teachers, and school leaders gain an incentive to customize class enrollment options and offer a wider variety of extracurricular opportunities to their students. Accountability contracts also enable teachers to formatively evaluate student performance by incorporating classroom assessments, reading and writing comprehension, and alternative measures of individual achievement.

My proposal to offer every single school system in Georgia the ability to enter into an accountability contract is grounded in the power of voluntary participation. When given the choice, most schools will weigh the advantages and receive overwhelmingly positive input from principals, teachers, and parents that will make them inclined to move forward and embrace a model for school-level management. Some school systems will face tough choices to determine how they can best organize and structure their approach to educating students; however, by appropriately addressing difficult issues directly, each school will have the ability to confront longstanding and far reaching inequalities. In the years ahead, innovation in schools across our state will transform the concept of public education as we know it.

It is impossible for a top-down system to account for the different needs of 1.7 million students across Georgia. Similarly, mandates that we impose on school systems aren't able to sidestep the wide variation that exists between the 159 counties in our state of more than 10 million people.[55] Still, some will question, *"Why should our state government give up any of the power and control we have over these school systems?"* Simply put, each of our systems—

and often the schools that make up systems—have widely different needs and concerns. One of our state's greatest strengths is our diversity. Upon closer examination, it's easy to understand why a large and diverse group of schools will benefit from adopting localized governance structures and operating under school-level management. Nevertheless, it will take time and an extensive process of preparation for all of our school systems to successfully transition into operating independently.

CHARTER SYSTEMS:
INNOVATION IN PUBLIC EDUCATION

In the first section of this chapter, I explained why I believe that it will remain impossible for the state of Georgia to implement a vision for what the purpose of our public education system should be until we give local schools the authority to individually control their operations. An accountability contract with the state of Georgia can be tailored to meet the needs and capabilities of any single school system and will, therefore, offer the most generally accessible path to school-level governance for every school in the state. It will take effort and compromise, but we should not be afraid to lose anything by empowering all of our schools to become more independent. Earlier, I asked the question: *With respect to the outcome for individual students, what is the purpose of public education?* Once we recognize that individual schools can capably manage themselves, we can challenge ourselves to reject the status quo by redefining the value of public education.

Education issues are sometimes framed as a choice between improving our entire statewide system, and descending into a free-for-all with no rules or safeguards. In part, a false choice is presented because public education is funded and administered through a structure that cannot be compared to any public or private institution. Federal, state, and local governments have all disjointedly assumed involvement in public education—causing us to collectively marginalize and overlook each school's ability to educate individual students. It might sound counterintuitive that a voluntary contract—which expands each school's decision-making authority—will solve longstanding problems in the continuity of our education system. But abandoning a top-down approach to public education will permit schools to redefine expectations for student learning and academic advancement more in line with reality. After we adopt a baseline governance system for schools to assume accountability over decision-making, we should do everything possible to encourage and promote innovation in public education.

While many teachers do incorporate computers, projectors, and other forms of technology to instruct students, we have not come close to systematically modernizing our education system. Incorporating technology into public education will be much more challenging than simply providing access to different types of technology in our classrooms. School systems across our state must confront the arduous challenge of comprehensively reforming their operations. For some systems, this will mean reevaluating the manner in which they carry out every major organizational function and asking how our objectives in education are being advanced by each of their expenditures.

In 1998, I worked with an organizing group of business people to form a community bank called Southern Heritage. Southern Hall County, which comprises 60 percent of Hall County's population, did not have access to a locally owned bank with the mission of serving our community. I became the chairman of the board of directors for Southern Heritage when we were granted our charter as a bank, and I assumed a very active role in the decision-making process to guide Southern Heritage to success. We were successful, and our community bank grew to hold millions of dollars in assets.

Community banks offer an irreplaceable function to people across our state because they incorporate a human element into banking, which gives them the unparalleled ability to find creative financial solutions that help people move forward. We accepted an offer to merge with Gainesville Bank and Trust after our board determined that it would provide the best opportunity for our bank to better serve our customers and shareholders. One of the main reasons that we decided to merge with Gainesville Bank and Trust was because we liked their model of governance.

By operating as a holding company, Gainesville Bank and Trust created a model where they continued to let each bank have its own identity under an independent board of directors. Our bank retained the ability to review loans, and our board maintained extensive decision-making authority to advance our mission of serving southern Hall County. We improved our ability to offer access to capital in our community. Furthermore, we operated more efficiently by consolidating our administrative activities within our larger holding company. I joined the board of directors for Gainesville Bank and Trust's holding company. For several years, I served on the board as our bank continued its expansion.

When I started to think critically about governance in education, I made an important connection to my experience as the chairman of the board in a community bank. Before Southern Heritage could begin operating, we had to raise a significant amount of capital from investors, and submitted an application to the state of Georgia to be granted a state bank charter. Southern Heritage had to demonstrate that we had a reasonable chance to serve our community's needs before we could qualify for a charter. To prove our viability, we were required to formulate a detailed plan that explained how we would meet our primary responsibilities, and that we possessed enough capital to support the functions of our bank. Once our charter was installed, Southern Heritage was able to support a significant level of economic development in southern Hall County and provide access to financial resources for many of our residents, just as we promised.

After I won the general election in 2006, and as I began to think about the fact that I would soon take office as Georgia's next lieutenant governor, I felt a sense of personal responsibility to do everything in my power to improve public education. Even in those communities with the resources to support collaborative governance models, local schools are not utilizing assets that could benefit their students. There are countless parents in our state who are watching their children receive an education they know is not good enough. *So what are we going to do about it?* Part of the solution will be to offer individual schools a way to develop innovative programs to provide new choices and academic opportunities for students.

In 2007, I worked with legislators in the General Assembly to pass the Charter Systems Act, which formally allowed school districts to voluntarily enter into a five-year contractual agreement with the state of Georgia.[56] To become a charter system, districts are required to articulate operable goals and outline a strategic plan to implement and manage a local system of governance. To be granted a charter, each school district must clearly define its objectives, benchmarks, and methods of evaluation it will follow.[57] For a charter system to succeed, school leadership structures must incorporate principals, teachers, parents, and valuable members of each community.

Under the charter system's accountability contract, first-year scores on the College and Career Readiness Performance Index are used to establish a baseline of academic performance. In the second year as part of a charter system, schools seek to meet or exceed the average CCRPI scores, both in their local district and statewide. In years three through five, schools focus on implementing academic programs and innovations that will allow their students to reach new heights in academic achievement.[58]

Adopting a charter system allows elementary, middle, and high schools to coordinate their operations. This lets schools operate more efficiently by consolidating administrative functions, while also giving primary and secondary school teachers the ability to work in sync through a system network. Each school within a charter system maintains its own governance board, giving it flexibility to creatively design new instructional programs.

When the Charter Systems Act was introduced in 2007, we confronted resistance from lobbyists and members of the educational establishment who argued that charter systems should not be granted the ability to deviate from the majority of state mandates. However, it is critical to empower school-level leaders and, most importantly, teachers, so that they can deliver the best possible outcomes to their students. Other individuals argued that we shouldn't allow charter systems to waive state mandates for the salary schedule of public school teachers. But if individual systems don't have the flexibility to determine how much to pay teachers, then we are indicating to teachers that they are simply employees of the government and should follow the status quo formula.

We have to do everything possible to create a culture inside our public schools of providing all of our students with access to the materials and resources needed to realize individual success. To stop negative behavior from occurring, teachers and local leaders have to develop relationships with students. To develop more relationships with students, our commonly-held values have to become stronger. For our values to strengthen, norms in public schools will have to change. Norms change with culture, and if we want the culture in our schools to become more positive, school climate is the first thing we have to improve. We should give teachers, school counselors, and supporting faculty members the tools they need to address discipline issues early and effectively by identifying the source of each student's individual problems and helping him or her to move forward by focusing on learning.

One exemplary innovation that several of our state's charter systems have demonstrated to be effective is the Georgia Department of Education's Climate Star Ratings Program, which is impacted by the Positive Behavioral Interventions and Supports (PBIS) system.[59] PBIS has proven to serve as an effective framework for improving school climate in a way that will positively impact academic outcomes, improve attendance, and reduce disciplinary referrals. In addition to maintaining a positive school climate, providing access to identification and intervention methods early on in elementary and middle schools has been shown to help minimize the prevalence of disciplinary problems among older students, leading to better overall academic outcomes.

Positive Behavioral Interventions and Supports—Proactive
and Interactive Strategies:
School Climate Star Rating Data Metrics (School Climate Star
Rating (Scale 1-5: Negative to Positive)

25%	25%	25%	25%
Student Survey	Student Discipline	School-wide Attendance	Survey +
Parent Survey		(Students, teachers,	Discipline
School Staff Survey		faculty)	(Ratio of
			drugs, alcohol,
			bullying, & dangerous
			incidents)

In schools across Georgia, P.E. teachers are often the highest paid instructors because they also perform duties as a coach.[60] This allows them to earn supplements that are not available to those in traditional academic subjects. These supplements often come from booster clubs and private organizations, which raise additional sources of funding to support extracurricular programming. I appreciate the value of P.E. classes, and without advice from my coaches in high school, I would not be the person that I am today. But the teachers who help our students learn advanced concepts must be appropriately compensated in line with the market value of their skills. Mandatory teacher salary schedules are part of the reason that many schools cannot attract talented individuals who are employed in the private sector to accept jobs in public schools.

In Marietta City Schools, one of its charter system reforms was to create a new incentive for its teachers to pursue advanced degrees.[61] Under this program, teachers can apply for tuition assistance to go back to school and earn advanced degrees receiving reimbursement of up to $20,000 for tuition. Approval is not automatic, and Marietta's City Schools place a strong preference towards math, science, special education, and language arts teachers. Upon earning advanced degrees from the program, teachers will earn a \$12,000 retention bonus, dispersed over four years. If they don't use all \$20,000 in tuition assistance, half of the unused portion will be added back to the retention bonus.

Allowing principals and local leaders to govern our schools empowers teachers, increases effectiveness and transparency in budgeting funds, and affirms the right of valuable members of each community to contribute to their schools. Charter systems allow each community to contribute directly to schools, giving students access to the best resources available. Over almost a decade, we have continued to make significant progress in growing our network of charter systems across the state of Georgia. When the 2016–17 school year begins, forty charter systems will be operating. Ranging in size from Warren County, with approximately 600 students, to Fulton County's more than 90,000 students, in total, more than 325,000 students will be enrolled in a charter system.[62]

Since our state introduced the concept of charter systems, the results have been extraordinary. When I listen to educators, school leaders, and superintendents describe how flexibility from mandates and local governance teams can be used to strengthen their neighborhoods—making schools the central engines of activity, resources, and development—it inspires me to work even harder on behalf of the students who will benefit each and every day. Watching systems from Atlanta Public Schools to Clarke County transition into charter systems gives me renewed optimism that Georgia's brightest days lie ahead.

6

Why Industry Matters

As we look ahead into the next century, leaders will be those who empower others.[63]

—Bill Gates

One of the hardest things for politicians to talk about, in practical terms, is what the American Dream means today. We know that all students in Georgia are capable of imagining a rewarding future and dream of living with purpose, and it is disappointing to me that the American Dream is often talked about as something that's not attainable for everybody. If an elected office-holder is discussing the subject, it's frequently dismissed as improbable that they will actually do anything to help people achieve their dreams. Otherwise, it's mutually acknowledged that the office-holder is using the American Dream to channel a campaign theme. In fairness, it is easy to get lost in lofty rhetoric when discussing something as far-reaching as the hopes and dreams of all Americans. But talking about the American Dream is necessary in order to frame the broader challenges our students face, which should make reforming public education a paramount obligation for every elected representative.

Americans in communities across our nation are asking the question: *If people have dreams everywhere, what makes the American Dream special?* Thankfully, we have not reached the point at which the notion of the American Dream is deemed offensive, but it is becoming exclusive—and for too many people, our nation's promise of hope has lost much of its meaning. The sentiment that the phrase "The American Dream" brings forth in the minds of people, both across country and across the world, even if they do not believe that it applies to them, is real.

If someone doubts that the children living in poverty in each of Georgia's 159 counties have dreams that they want to dedicate themselves to pursuing, and which they have the potential to realize, then that person is choosing to ignore reality for the purpose of fulfilling a stereotype. People everywhere can and should be able to achieve their dreams. But the American Dream has always gone further to represent our nation's optimism for the future. In practice, we have continued to make a substantial investment to provide a good education to all of our state's students. This is why the majority of funds that the state of Georgia appropriates each year are for public education, and why most of that money directly follows students to the school districts in which they are enrolled.

The education we obtain is vitally important to our lives. When every person is able to pursue individual goals to advance as far as his or her abilities will take them, then the freedoms and rights our government guarantees will be fully realized. Working should give people the capacity to earn an income to provide for themselves and their families, enabling them to follow and experience their own dreams. That is what all parents want for their children, and what provides more fulfillment than anything else: the ability to be self-sufficient and to exercise ownership in determining the outlook of your own future.

I understand what the American Dream means because I have lived it. However, in my experience, the things that have impacted the direction of my life most have rarely gone according to plan.

Our economy rewards individuals who use their abilities and creativity in business, permitting entrepreneurs to share in the successes of the world's most dynamic industries. Every day, businesses grant individuals new pathways to achieving something significant. Companies across our state have created remarkable value by producing goods and services that make our economy grow, bringing millions of jobs to the state of Georgia. No company is perfect, just as there is no single definition of success, but I believe in the power of foundational skills, enterprise, and free markets. It is my hope that we never lose sight of the value that job creators add to our society. At the same time, we must give equal respect to every person for the work that he or she does to earn a living. A welder and a philosophy instructor both are employed in honorable professions. However, one should not be viewed as any more important in our society because both jobs provide individuals with the ability to help create a sustainable economy. We should always strive to place dignity in the value of honest work, irrespective of income or job title.

GEORGIA'S COLLEGE AND CAREER ACADEMIES

At the onset of my career, I learned one of the most important components—if not the most vital factor—in determining whether or not a business will succeed. A business owner must strategically invest for the future they want to realize. It is incredibly easy for an undercapitalized business to cut its way to closing its doors permanently. Most businesses that fail in America do so because they lack access to the necessary level of capital to operate for long enough to grow and become profitable.[64] When I make the statement that I have experienced the American Dream, few people doubt my sincerity. Unfortunately, too many people believe that I am the exception to the rule, and they do not believe that in their own futures they will achieve anything close to my personal outcome of success. This is unacceptable.

In fact, I cannot claim that the experiences, which have led me to write this book, are the product of my being a straight-A student. But I do believe that my success is the product of hard work. I was blessed to have a mother who taught me the value of hard work, and who was willing to take a second mortgage out on her home to help me pursue a dream. But if we went back in time to statistically capture my performance using today's standards when I was a student at South Hall Middle School or Johnson High School, I imagine that I wouldn't be close to what our system now generally considers as a student who is on a trajectory toward academic and professional success. In reality, I struggled to consistently make Bs. When I did, it was usually because of exceptional teachers who put as much effort as necessary into teaching me the concepts I needed to learn.

I have often felt as though I can relate to the perspectives of the many students who are being failed by our education system. For example, I understand why some students struggle to find relevance in what they learn year after year. When I was in school, I always felt more like a kid who was picturing what I wanted to be when I grew up, instead of preparing for a practical career in my future. From my point of view, when I woke up every day, athletics and football practice were what made me excited to go to school.

I don't admit this to be bashful of academic success or to send students the wrong message that they don't need to challenge themselves academically to achieve their goals. Education is the most important investment that anyone can make. But I want to be honest about my academic performance (which was not remarkable) because it's part of what motivates me to relentlessly put forward the greatest possible effort to improve public education for every student in Georgia.

I also believe that I owe everything I have accomplished professionally to following the advice that Erk Russell gave me at Georgia Southern. Coach Russell proved to me that when I worked as hard as possible and used every minute of my time as effectively as I could, I had the ability to surpass any limitations confronting me.

Focused on jump-starting my career, I dedicated myself to working as hard as I could in everything that I did. I accepted every available job that I thought might lead to something bigger. I never expected that in less than two years, working at the Northeast Georgia Athletic Club would lead me to own, of all things, a formalwear business. But it did. With the help of my parents, I was able, at twenty-one years old to buy the business that became the foundation my career was built upon. Owning my own business motivated me to invest countless hours into each workweek. The more I worked, the more frequently I received new opportunities to advance professionally.

I have worked to advocate for system-wide education reform to allow individual school systems to take ownership over teaching all of our students. My ability to lead a statewide effort to improve public education is a direct consequence of the extraordinary development our state experienced in the decades immediately preceding the twenty-first century.

In 1966, the Atlanta Falcons football team was founded, and shortly thereafter, the Braves relocated to Georgia from Milwaukee, Wisconsin.[65] Two years later, in 1968, after departing St. Louis, Missouri, the Hawks joined both teams and made our state's capital their home.[66] These three athletic franchises have contributed billions to our state's economy over the past five decades. In addition to achieving many notable accomplishments, including an Atlanta Braves victory in the 1995 World Series, these teams have, more importantly, grown to represent our state's identity. Both the Falcons and the Braves doubled-down on their investment in Georgia when, in 2015, they broke ground on separate projects to build new stadiums in a multi-billion dollar construction effort.[67]

In the early 1970s, Birmingham, Alabama, and Atlanta, Georgia, had similar populations and nearly the same regional influence.[68] Nevertheless, it seems almost impossible to make a serious comparison between our two cities now. One of the biggest contributors to the tremendous economic growth that Georgia has realized over the last few decades is the investment that the City of Atlanta made to build Hartsfield-Jackson Atlanta International Airport. Historically, Atlanta first invested in building airport infrastructure for public use in 1925.[69] In 1961, Atlanta spent $21 million on construction for the largest airport terminal in the US, which was capable of accommodating more than six million people each year.[70] In 1977, Mayor Maynard Jackson led the City of Atlanta forward in a lasting and historic expansion of our airport. We built what was then recorded as the largest construction project ever completed in the South at a total cost of more than $500 million.[71] Since 1998, Atlanta's airport has remained the world's busiest. Annually, Hartsfield-Jackson serves more than 95 million passengers and approximately one million flights from all over the world.

When we appreciate the strategic investments that the state of Georgia has made in our future, it becomes clear why we have advanced so quickly and why we remain positioned to experience untold growth in our future. In the 1980s and 1990s, Atlanta rapidly became a metropolitan magnet.[72] Not only were we competing with other cities in the Southeast, we soon gained national attention that would ignite a global response to Atlanta's rising claim as one of the greatest cities in the world.

Oftentimes, individuals with loud voices call negative attention to MARTA, the Metro-Atlanta public transit system, and declare that it is outdated and unnecessary. To be fair, MARTA has overcome its share of operational challenges and turned around its business model in recent years—and much work still remains to be done[73]—but if we didn't have both MARTA and the Hartsfield-Jackson Atlanta International Airport, I don't think Atlanta would have been chosen to host the 1996 Olympics. Our leaders, both public and private, had the foresight to know that Georgia was capable of achieving just as much success as any other major city in the world and, as a result, they made all the necessary investments in our future.

In 1996, Georgia's success was acknowledged worldwide when Atlanta was honored with a distinction shared by only two cities in America to host the Summer Olympics.[74] Our Olympic slogan of "Come Celebrate Our Dream," reflected how remarkable Georgia had grown. In a spotlight before people everywhere, Atlanta demonstrated the strength of our state's diversity, the economic productivity, and the entrepreneurial ingenuity that made us the economic center of the Southeast. There are many examples of strategic investments started by individuals planting seeds and having faith that they would grow and become unbelievably and distinctly successful. The mission of public education must be for each of our schools to continually foster that same type of investment within every student in Georgia.

Unfortunately, our public education system has not yet come close to capitalizing on the extraordinary potential that exists due to our state's natural, economic, and human resources. In the early 2000s, approximately 60 percent of students in Georgia were graduating from high school.[75] Everyone recognized that this was unacceptably low. We were confronted with the fact that hundreds of thousands of people were entering our state's workforce with neither a high school diploma nor employable skills. We also needed to improve the quality of our education system to give value to the degrees that students earned when they did graduate. It has since been proven that these objectives are one in the same, and they are exceptionally difficult to achieve within high schools using a status quo four-year academic program.

As all kids get older, one of the questions they can count on being asked repeatedly is: *What do you want to be when you grow up?* We should expect, as most students learn and gain more experience, that they are going to develop different interests and, correspondingly, change career goals. However, too many people are graduating from high school and college without a plan for the future. As a result, thousands of recent college graduates are now faced with a choice between being unemployed or over-qualified for a job that does not require their degree.[76] Enabling students to continue onto a successful career after graduation will require our schools to provide them with meaningful opportunities to explore and apply their academic interests at an earlier age.

The Red and Black, an independent student newspaper based in Athens, Georgia, published an article in June 2014 titled, "College graduates may delay careers facing today's job market."[77] The article cites data from the University of Georgia Career Center to indicate that: "62 percent of the class of 2013 reported working a full-time job six months after graduation, while 38 percent of students reported underemployment and unemployment." Before discussing why it has become more common for students to postpone a career to undergo additional skills training, the article asks: "Do degrees really matter?"

How will our state combat the fact that 38 percent of graduates from our flagship university are unable to find good jobs? Statistics tell us that 7 out of 10 people will need marketable technical skills to get a job in the twenty-first century economy.[78] It is imperative that we approach education reform with a sense of urgency, because every day that we wait, millions of people feel the consequences. The fact that our state has an aging workforce should not cause us to worry about how we will find the required number of people to fill the skilled jobs of those who are retiring. In a state like Georgia, with the eighth-largest population in the US[79] and a dynamic economy driven by Atlanta, we should be excited at the prospect of allowing the next generation to lead us to new heights.

After I was sworn in as Georgia's lieutenant governor in January 2007, one of my highest priorities was to give every high school student, as well as individuals in communities across our state, access to local institutions offering accredited post-secondary courses and technical certification programs. When I visited Coweta County schools, I discovered a model that I knew had potential to work in every community across the state. Coweta County was responding to a real workforce demand brought on by an existing industry.

They watched a locally based job creator choose to expand in another state instead of bringing new jobs to their county. *Why?* The company could not find the workforce they needed to be successful. Instead of accepting the status quo, Coweta County officials joined with education leaders and moved forward with a new plan. They used the charter school law to find the flexibility needed to create new education pathways, and they tore down traditional education silos to create a unique learning environment, blending a high school campus with the local technical college. Their focus was workforce development, and they demonstrated this commitment by putting their school's governance board in communication with many of the community's business leaders. Coweta County's collective response was to overwhelmingly embrace this new structure for public education.

All high school students are now given the choice to leave their base high school and attend the Central Educational Center (CEC) to take advantage of post-secondary coursework that is relevant to their professional goals, meeting the needs of a diverse set of industries in west Georgia. I knew that this model had significant potential for success, so I put together a statewide plan and created an incentive program to help communities build what I called "College and Career Academies." I envisioned College and Career Academies as an extension of individual public school systems, but which could operate as part of an interconnected network of workforce development engines across Georgia. I wanted to establish a model that we could replicate, while allowing each College and Career Academy to adjust its programs to better meet the academic and workforce development needs of its respective community.

I did not invent the underlying concepts behind College and Career Academies, but I worked to develop a strategy to grow College and Career Academies into economic engines for communities across our state. What I saw being developed in Coweta County was the spark that allowed me to predict how College and Career Academies could transform workforce development and post-secondary education in Georgia. From that point forward, I focused my attention on improving that model's reach and potential effectiveness by making College and Career Academies into a cohesive statewide program. I set out to accomplish a clear and overarching objective: to build new College and Career Academies so that we could duplicate one program's success for more students.

I officially established the College and Career Academy Network in 2007, and every year since, we have offered a larger number of competitive grants for new school systems to begin construction on a College and Career Academy.[80] I made sure that the characteristics of a best practice academy were codified in Georgia law so that we could move high schools across our state forward. College and Career Academies represent a community partnership between a local school system, a partnering technical college, and business leaders represented on the academy's governing board to ensure the fulfillment of its workforce development mission—specific to each community.

In 2007, I persuaded the General Assembly to appropriate $15 million in the state budget to establish a competitive grant process to help school systems build College and Career Academies.[81] With a typical construction cost of $9–12 million, our $3 million incentive generated enough attention to attract a considerable number of competitive applications. I wanted to find public schools with leaders who were serious about reforming their schools and who would be committed to using the full potential of a College and Career Academy to transform their community.

In our first year, we awarded five grants to school systems in different areas throughout our state, which committed to begin construction on College and Career Academies immediately.[82] I made it my goal that by the year 2020, every single student in Georgia would have access to a College and Career Academy. In the last decade, we have made notable progress. Although much remains to be done, my objective has not changed in the years since. In the 2016–17 school year, more than 15,000 students will enroll in Georgia's thirty-seven College and Career Academies.[83] Plans are in place for more school systems to receive grants each year, making it possible for them to build their own College and Career Academies.

I have been part of enough economic development meetings and presentations with CEOs and business leaders to understand that when a company chooses a new site to expand its operations, one of the first questions that its leadership is guaranteed to ask is: *How can we be assured that our workforce will have access to a quality public education system that will attract families to move to this community?* For Georgia to continue attracting industry and diversifying our economy, we have to find a way to produce a workforce with the technical skills that companies are demanding in the twenty-first century. Each individual College and Career Academy represents an investment in the infrastructure necessary to support our state's economic development and workforce training needs in the future.

College and Career Academies are an acknowledgment by our state's education system that industry matters. In return for the billions of dollars that we invest in public education, we should expect our schools to produce a skilled workforce capable of adapting to meet the demands of any new industry that moves to Georgia. College and Career Academies give school systems the ability to support higher growth for existing businesses and new businesses that locate to their respective communities. One such example exists in Madison County, where its College and Career Academy works closely with Athens Technical College.[84] Madison County's College and Career Academy operates by educating students under a school mantra of 3-Rs: rigor, relevance, and relationships. Madison College and Career Academy's governing leaders established a relationship with the Caterpillar manufacturing plant in Athens, where a group of high school students have since worked as summer interns.

Empowering each public school with independent decision-making authority will give us the ability to ensure that every single community in our state is capable of developing a skilled workforce, which can meet the demands of any industry with a College and Career Academy. College and Career Academies afford public schools, businesses, and higher education institutions with the ability to partner in two mutually fundamental goals: growing communities and increasing our state's economic productivity. The state of Georgia has one of the most diverse economies in America. Our state's geographic location, climate, and natural resources will facilitate the environment necessary for our agricultural industry to be productive far into our future. However, nothing will grow our entire economy more than strengthening Georgia's public education system by giving schools the ability to make sure that the financial resources, which are appropriated on a per-capita student basis by the state, are most effectively spent in our classrooms and on individual students.

College and Career Academies are designed to be genuine economic engines, and must maintain an active partnership with local businesses and economic development leaders in the community. Each school system's leaders must also recognize that offering a high quality education to its students requires them to incorporate input from both teachers and business leaders. If schools can identify what industries need, and if businesses can contribute to helping students gain the skills they require to qualify for good jobs, then we can meaningfully connect our public education system to the reality of the economic and professional outlook that students will face after graduating from high school.

In 2016, I worked with the leaders of Coweta County's College and Career Academy to introduce another major innovation that will push Georgia to the forefront of transforming public education as we know it. Partnering with the German American Chamber of Commerce, we launched the Georgia Consortium for Advanced Technical Training (GA CATT)—the nation's first true German-style apprenticeship for high school students. Under the inaugural program at Coweta County's Central Education Center, 10th grade students will have the opportunity to enroll in a course of study that allows them to earn a high school diploma, German apprenticeship certificate, and an associate degree in Industrial Mechanics from West Georgia Technical College—all within their regular graduation timeline. To form their GA CATT program, eight local manufacturing companies partnered with Coweta County schools. Participating students combine traditional high school classes, manufacturing training courses and apprenticeship modules that will pay $8 dollars an hour in each student's first year. By the time students reach 12th grade, they will spend 80% of their time learning at a manufacturing site, while earning $12 an hour. Because of the German model's unique delivery system, designed by the chamber of commerce to incorporate input from businesses, GA CATT is a clear demonstration of how education drives the economy. Part of the reason that reforming our public education system is so important is because of the central role schools play in the lives of millions of children throughout our state. When students attend classes, interact with teachers, or join athletic teams and extracurricular organizations, they develop an intensely personal relationship with their schools and greater communities.

Since our state began investing in College and Career Academies in 2007, I have made an effort to visit their campuses as often as possible. I will never forget one visit I made to the Athens Community Career Academy in 2013 because that's when I met Jasmine Kidd. Her determination to earn a bright future continues to inspire me to work as hard as I can to provide every high school student with access to a College and Career Academy. Today, Jasmine attends Georgia State University and is on track to graduate in May 2018 with a pre-law focus. In the next section, I'll let Jasmine tell her own story. I hope that her success in the face of personal adversity inspires others to realize that there is nothing more powerful than unleashing an individual's potential.

STUDENT-BY-STUDENT SUCCESS

By Jasmine Kidd

My name is Jasmine Kidd, and I was born on October 9, 1996, in Decatur, Georgia. When I was growing up, my family moved from home to home because my parents were always looking for better jobs so our family could make ends meet. When things got tough or I thought about giving up, and sometimes I did, I've always been motivated to move past any doubts about the future because I know that no matter what happens, I will still have God, my family, and an education.

From kindergarten through twelfth grade, I attended five elementary schools, five middle schools, and two high schools. Looking back, my memories about going to school are mostly organized by location, because where I went to school revolved around where we were living at the time. My mom and dad have made their careers in the fast-food industry, and we moved whenever my parents got better job opportunities. At times, we relocated so frequently that it was difficult to adjust to a new school and home, let alone think about anything else. Sometimes, if we moved during the middle of a school year, my mom and dad would make an extra effort to drive me to the bus stop each morning and pick me up in the afternoon so that I could graduate, uninterrupted, before transferring to a new school. That was the case when I went to Swint Elementary in fourth grade, moved, and later transferred to Calloway Elementary to start the fifth grade.

Beyond adjusting to new schools, I didn't always find it easy to get used to other less-than-ideal aspects of our living arrangements, which usually weren't in the best of conditions. I'll never forget the image of the orange-ish, brownish Pittsburgh Apartment complex, located near downtown Atlanta, where we lived in the early 2000s. It was because of my experiences there at six years old that I decided, in my future, I wanted to help people by fighting to represent what's right.

Like everyone, I've learned different lessons from the high and low points I have experienced. For example, when I went to Bethune Elementary School, our family shared a big yellow house on Kennedy Street. The house had six bedrooms, a huge kitchen and dining room, and a very spacious den. It was the place where I liked living the most. But when I was eight years old, we had to move to Riverdale because my parents felt that it was time for a change. Unfortunately for our family, the day after we moved into our new apartment, our previous house was robbed. They took everything that we had, even the thermostat. Seeing our family lose so much of what my parents had worked extremely hard to earn, at eight years old, I made a promise to myself that when I had a family of my own, I would do everything that I could to provide us with a better life. Because of my awareness of how important it is to become successful in my future, I've never let anything draw my attention away from working hard to get good grades in school.

More than once, I remember my dad telling me, "I don't want you to be like me; I want you to be better than me." He didn't say that because he wasn't providing properly for our family; he'd say it because he wanted nothing but the best for my future. I know that my mom and dad worked a lot of very long hours to give me the opportunity for a successful future. My parents were honest and direct with me about how important it is to get a good education because they wanted me to avoid the stress that worrying about your next paycheck can put on a parent. When my mom and dad explained to me why they didn't graduate from college, and how difficult it made looking for a job, I told them that I wouldn't let anything stop me from earning a diploma.

My family moved to Athens near the end of my eighth-grade year, and that's when I first heard about College and Career Academies. The CEO of the Athens College and Career Academy, Ms. Arrowood, visited my English class at Hilsman Middle School and told us that we could start college early if we enrolled there after we turned sixteen.

I knew that I wanted to go to college, but up to that point, I had the mindset that I would need to graduate from high school before I could think about graduating from college. When Ms. Arrowood said that criminal justice was one of the career pathways offered at the Athens College and Career Academy, I knew that I wanted to go there. At the end of my tenth grade year, while I was attending Cedar Shoals High School, my family moved to the west side of Athens. I was given the choice of staying full-time as a student at Clarke Central High School or applying to the Athens College and Career Academy. It wasn't a difficult choice, and after taking the Compass test and qualifying to take college-level classes at the Athens Community Career Academy, I enrolled full-time during my junior and senior years. Over two years of taking classes, I earned 44 credit hours, which will count towards the degree I am now pursuing at Georgia State University.

I think that attending a College and Career Academy during my last two years of high school prepared me for the challenges of being a college student, both academically and in terms of better managing my time, making important decisions for my future independently, and thinking critically. English 1101 is one class that was tremendously helpful in preparing me for college. At the beginning of the school year, I thought I was a good writer and didn't think the semester would be much of a challenge. But after I turned in my first essay, my teacher, Mr. Dixon, told me he knew I could do better and that the course would help me to become a better writer. He taught me how to move past writing at a high-school level, and my performance improved with every essay that I wrote. By the end of the year, not only had my grades on Mr. Dixon's papers improved by more than one letter grade, but I'd also become more comfortable with writing, and found out that it helped me with other subject matters, too.

As a college student, I think the things that I learned at the Athens Community Career Academy that are most beneficial to me now at Georgia State were the demonstrations of how different subjects, like math and psychology, come together in real life and allow us to understand life more deeply. Many of my teachers also gave me personal attention, and that motivated me to move outside of my comfort zone and take classes in subjects that I had struggled with in previous years, like biology or algebra.

I know I am prepared to be successful at Georgia State. At the same time, I am ready to take on the new challenges that I will face with each passing day, as I get closer to pursuing my dreams in the real world. Although I haven't decided exactly what type of law I am going to specialize in, and I can't say exactly where I'll be in my future, I am excited to be exploring different classes in college that are helping me gain more confidence that my chosen career path of becoming an attorney is right for me. No matter what, I know that as long as I keep my faith strong and continue to work hard in all of my classes, good things will keep helping to guide me in the future.

7

Disruption

We cannot solve problems by using the same kind of thinking
we used when we created them.[85]

—Albert Einstein

I was born in 1966. Today, Georgia is a strikingly different place
than it was when I was a child. The world has changed a great
deal; however, our progress continues to be driven by the same
core factors: a growing and diverse population, our state's abun-
dant resources and geographical advantages, and effective leaders
who can make decisions to capitalize on Georgia's potential. Our
state has changed for the better, and disrupting the established
way of doing things has repeatedly proven to make us stronger.

In recent decades, technology has transformed our economy,
and in many respects altered life as we know it. We live in the digital age. Today in America, there are more cellphones than there
are people. Even as we embrace new innovations, we cannot forget
how far and how quickly we have advanced in the past decade.

On the other hand: *what are the biggest changes that have occurred in our public education system over the past twenty years?* The
standardized tests we use to measure performance and aptitude,
the physical buildings where our students learn, and the digitaliza-
tion of some textbooks and instructional materials are the most
obvious examples. The progress being made by public schools
pales in comparison to the level of innovation occurring within our
economy. Rarely does our education system reward progress in
individual schools, or successfully identify and promote exceptionally innovative programs to a wider audience of schools. Instead,
we hardly make it much farther than discussing what it would be

like if public schools innovated in the first place. Simply put, we have to set higher goals. To do so, we must acknowledge that the only way to realize our objectives in public education is to believe in the potential of principals, teachers, parents, and students and to include them as part of the economic and workforce development engines in our communities.

Vast differences exist between Georgia's 2,300 public schools. Under our current system, some perform extraordinarily well, most are average, and some are failing their students. Perhaps most importantly, our one-size-fits-all system has historically failed to align what Georgia's students learn in public schools with what the best and highest paying jobs in our state require. If our workforce cannot meet existing demand for high-skilled jobs or provide a sufficient number of applicants to replace those who are retiring, as is the case today, we will never achieve anything close to our potential.

To frame the challenges that we face in reforming public education, it is imperative to understand how our economy responds to real examples of change. Approximately 107 years after Alexander Graham Bell dialed the first telephone call in 1876, Motorola offered the first cellphone for sale to the general public.[86] I purchased my first cellphone, a Motorola Bag Phone, while I was working to expand my first business in the late 1980s. In 2016, 33 years after the first cellphones went into commercial distribution, not only is it exceedingly difficult to imagine life without cellphones, but most of today's cellphones no longer function as just mobile phones. Instead, they utilize a wireless network infrastructure that gives us near limitless access to information and a wide array of products and services on the Internet. In recent years, smartphones have become a public platform through which applications are developed and made available for sale, and in many cases for free, to an estimated two billion people—satisfying an increasing number of new consumer demands each day.[87]

When I was growing up, we had a family friend named Raymond Kinney. He worked at BellSouth, the regulated phone company that served Georgia at the time. Our families attended church together, and I admired Raymond as someone with an incredibly exciting and rewarding career. I will never forget a conversation I had with him at our family's home in the early 1980s. We sometimes found out from him about new development projects that were being proposed in Georgia. I was always interested in learning about the new technologies, even if I didn't fully appreciate their significance in the long term. But what Raymond told us that night went beyond anything I could have previously imagined.

Usually, Raymond told us about projects related to infrastructure. We could conceptualize what he was explaining in terms of how it would look physically. This time, he told us something different. On that night, Raymond was visibly excited as he started to describe what BellSouth and other telecommunication companies were exploring. I vividly remember him setting the stage for the information that he was about to share, saying: "You will never believe what we're working on."

Raymond explained that in the future, people would stop communicating with telephones—or at least do so a lot less frequently. He sat on the couch next to me and explained that instead of talking to each other on the phone, one day we would be able to sit at a desk, look into a screen, and talk face-to-face with people anywhere in the world. He said it would be like the way that we were talking right then, and similar to watching TV but with a live line of communication being transmitted between two receivers. Needless to say, Raymond was correct and today video communication technology is widely available on most computers and cellphones. Cellphones have also surpassed cameras as the primary devices used by most people to take pictures and videos. It took a huge stretch of my imagination to comprehend the reality of what he was telling us. In the early 1980s, the notion of someone developing a program like Skype or FaceTime seemed extremely far-fetched and ambitious.

As I reflect on the visionary idea that Raymond Kinney posited when I was a teenager—in the context of my life in 2016—I am reminded of great moments in our nation's history when we challenged ourselves to accomplish something extraordinary. We are overdue for such a challenge in public education. When President John F. Kennedy announced on May 25, 1961 that America would send an astronaut to the moon before the decade's end, many people doubted his vision. Nevertheless, on July 20, 1969, Neil Armstrong stepped off of the Apollo 11 spacecraft and famously announced to the world that President Kennedy's dream—which captivated a generation of Americans—had been fulfilled: "One small step for man, one giant leap for mankind."[88] Our history holds thousands of examples of innovation and remarkable progress, which along with the deeply ingrained values that make our nation great, have contributed to the origin of the American Dream and elevated the United States of America as a worldwide force of leadership.

Now, established businesses can remain dominant only if they use their capital advantage to invest heavily in research and development or if they acquire small businesses that innovate. In any case, successful companies constantly look for every viable opportunity to gain a greater market share over their competitors. Competition is the entrepreneurial phenomenon that creates change. Businesses will change as quickly as possible if it means making more money. About a decade after I bought my Motorola Bag Phone, I purchased a computer. Since the turn of the twenty-first century, I have transitioned from using a flip phone, to a Blackberry, to an iPhone, and today, I have a Moto X second generation, which uses an operating system powered by Google.

According to the 2015 Forbes financial evaluation of global corporations, the three most valuable brands in the world are Apple, Microsoft, and Google. These companies are collectively worth more than $280 billion.[89] The massive growth experienced by these industries is a direct reflection of their contributions to the technological transformation of our economy, which continues to take place.

In 2015, Apple—the world's most valuable company since 2012—spent more than $8 billion on research and development.[90] Spending a comparable amount to develop the technologies that Apple is working on would have been incomprehensible in the not-so-distant past. In addition to manufacturing iPods, cellphones, computers, tablets, and electronic accessories, Apple is quickly expanding its scope into different markets. For example, Apple recently launched a music-streaming service to compete with growing companies like Spotify, which introduced innovations that improved upon earlier forerunners such as Pandora.

In 2001, iTunes was created to give artists the ability to sell songs and albums in a digital marketplace. For a few years, it was remarkably successful. However, after several years of decline in consumer demand due to people downloading music elsewhere—sometimes using illegal websites such as Napster—Apple decided they could generate more revenue by launching a streaming service. Instead of making individual purchases, subscribers pay a flat monthly fee to listen to an unlimited number of songs with Apple Music. As music streaming subscriptions led by Spotify have become more popular, downloading music illegally has also lost much of its appeal. This is just one example of a billion-dollar market sustaining widespread change, declining, and then—in a relatively short period of time, due to new developments in technology—rebounding.[91]

Every day we should prepare to accept that something new will change and never go back to the way it used to be; technology has made it considerably easier to turn an idea into a business. In addition to changing the products and services offered for sale, companies are also changing how these products are advertised, sold, and delivered.

Google was founded in 1998 and has since transformed the way in which the world accesses information.[92] Today, Google regularly makes headlines because of efforts to develop a self-driving car.[93] The company eBooks has made millions of books—including almost every notable literary work—available anytime, anywhere because the books can be downloaded online. Video-streaming companies such as Netflix, Hulu, HBO, and some cable providers have made almost all movies and televised programs accessible online and are challenging conventional notions about how people watch the news, television, and movies. Facebook, Twitter, Instagram, and other social media sites have fundamentally altered the way that information and ideas are shared, while PayPal, eBay, and Amazon have changed the way in which we purchase products. A large sector of our economy is now online.

For decades, we have worked to create a competitive business environment in Georgia. Successful economies are defined by the capability of entrepreneurs to use common infrastructure to implement new ideas that better satisfy consumer demand, increase efficiency, or provide an economic benefit to citizens. In every sector of our economy, fast moving, efficient, and innovative competitors have taken advantage of industry shortfalls by strategically shifting to meet the new demands and more closely fit the lifestyles of our citizens. As our economy has regained strength, investments made in our state over the past decade have positioned us to sustain greater growth and economic development in the years ahead.

When innovative companies introduce new products or services that favorably disrupt an established marketplace to benefit consumers, their impact cannot be reversed. Uber is one such company having that effect. In exchange for disrupting the taxicab industry, Uber received an extraordinary amount of attention from different politicians. But many public officials have applied a transparently shallow analysis to assessing the significance of global passenger networks such as Uber and Lyft. These individuals fail to see observable trends within Uber's operations that will reach other industries in the future or that could be applied to different government programs and institutions to help them improve their operations and work in sync to accomplish overlapping objectives.

To determine whether or not Uber's business model is good for consumers, it is important to understand exactly how the company's drivers operate. Uber was founded as a global passenger network in 2009.[94] Uber's mission is to provide millions of people with access to near effortless, accountable and, if possible, 24/7 private transportation. Using a basic software application that is free to download, anyone with a smartphone in 159 cities in North America or in the 58 countries across the world where drivers currently operate, can request transportation within minutes. Passengers pay for rides using an electronic payment method registered to an Uber account. Different rates are charged depending on the individual city, but Uber's pricing system is designed to deliver competitive fares, in which a base rate is charged, and then a per-mile fee when driving, and a per-minute fee when idling, is applied.

Despite legal challenges filed by taxicab companies and government entities, Uber, Lyft, and other platform services have prevailed because of support from consumers and a willingness to adapt to operating within fair parameters to ensure public safety.[95] Seeking to capitalize on new opportunities for expansion, Uber is examining ways to improve on-demand delivery services for a variety of innovative products. For example, as a promotion in 2014, Uber sent registered nurses, at no cost, to deliver flu shots and prevention packs during flu season to businesses and homes in Boston, New York City, and Washington, DC.[96]

Uber's innovative entrance into our state's marketplace will help to make sure that people always have access to safe and reliable transportation. Although Uber is governed by fewer regulations than traditional taxicab companies, in no respect do its drivers work in an unregulated market. Before passengers are picked up, the Uber app provides a fare estimate, the driver's name and photo, license plate number, and rating.[97] At the end of a trip customers rate their drivers. Drivers who do not meet Uber's ratings and quality standards are no longer allowed to partner with the company.

After several years of watching their operations grow, in the 2015 legislative session a bipartisan group of legislators in Georgia's General Assembly worked with public safety experts and representatives from Uber and Lyft to pass a compromise—seeking to eliminate any legitimate concerns.

What really makes Uber's model different, however, and a great example for how the Department of Education can begin to promote new innovations that improve Georgia's statewide public education system in the future, is that Uber isn't a taxicab company, in the same way that school boards and the Department of Education aren't schools. Instead, Uber functions as a technology-based marketplace, where, upon receiving approval of a basic set of criteria, individuals who apply to become drivers work as entrepreneurs and serve consumers at their will. In critical areas such as law enforcement and public education, innovations in technology allow us to record critical information that can improve our lives. There is a broader concept that we can learn from Uber and apply to reforming our public education system: The most important variables in our state's public education system are students and we should view them as our customers. If we fail to do so, they may seek other options, which, for too many students, means dropping out.

Companies such as Uber have become tremendously successful by combining existing resources with technology to create a marketplace that provides an effective service to meet a common demand. To be successful, we have to use all of our state's resources in K-12 public education. This means we should incorporate institutions such as the University of Georgia and Georgia Institute of Technology into our public education system, along with every other school in our state's university and technical college systems. We should allow businesses to pair real workforce development programs that train prospective employees with College and Career Academies. Above all, we must give our public schools the freedom and flexibility to do the best they can for their students with every resource available to them. If we rise to meet the challenge of true education reform, we can make Georgia's public education system into a platform from which our schools can launch transformational innovations.

Innovation in Public Education

In some areas of employment, it seems fair to ask: *Does our economy drive education or does education drive our economy?* Without a doubt, it has remained a fact for a long time that the quality of our education and workforce training system drives our economy. This is evidenced by the modern history of economic growth in our state and across our country. Unfortunately, public schools, as 2,300 entities making up a single, statewide system, remain extremely segmented in their ability to maintain pace with new jobs being created in our economy.[98] This sounds contradictory, but a fundamental flaw in how our public schools facilitate workforce development has brought expectations for the value of a high school diploma down to an unacceptably low level. Today, our high schools are severely limiting the skills of our workforce and failing to prepare students for a future after graduation. If we do not adapt our public education system to function in the twenty-first century, if we continue to fail to challenge the status quo and if we are not preparing every single student to be successful, our once-successful public schools will fall further behind with each passing day.

There is a widespread misunderstanding of the purpose that standards serve due to incorrect information that has been communicated, dating back to the 1983 *Nation at Risk* report that was commissioned under President Reagan.[99] Sadly, even in 1983 there were warnings that, by many indications, our nation's public education system was in need of serious reform. The *Nation at Risk* report launched a thirty year education reform effort across the United States.[100] We moved from one set of benchmarks to another. Ultimately, the *Nation at Risk* report led to a movement away from measuring progress in education by focusing on inputs and toward evaluating outputs such as student outcomes. Examples of inputs in education include: teacher-student ratios, numbers of teachers and administrators, percent of funding dedicated to direct instruction, and total dollars spent on each budget category to measure academic achievement.

While the shift from inputs to outputs was a core component of changing our focus from adults to students, our failure to focus on providing teachers and principals with the freedom to simply do what they do best—exercise their craft to prepare our students for college or careers—has prevented innovations across our public education system from gaining any real momentum. Our public schools have been effectively paralyzed from changing structurally because many of our leaders have focused on arguing over specific standards and mandates instead of really talking about schools. The question now remains: *How can we move the national conversation on public education back to individual schools, classrooms, and students?*

When I approach the concept of academic standards, I think about setting minimum expectations. Many schools use standards to create a default bar for all students by averaging the standardized test scores required for promotion to the next grade level. For all practical purposes, we set a singular objective for the majority of students to work towards, at least until they reach high school. Thereby, we force students into a very narrow set of parameters to define academic achievement, which, historically, has set a very low standard for success. A recurring failure to adapt to changing dynamics in our society has become amplified within our public education system, causing schools to suffer from the same challenges faced by other establishment entities that operate under a legacy model.

The only way to shift our focus to student achievement in individual public schools is by restoring a human element to education and giving independent governance authority to principals, teachers, and each school's leadership. My vision for public education in Georgia's future does not include a common set of class-by-class, grade-by-grade academic standards to be used statewide. Although we must set higher goals, standards themselves can sometimes be a deterrent to student achievement and classroom innovation. In my experience studying best practices in public education, programs in schools that produce the most successful students as measured by graduation rates and long term career placement are never driven by a single set of standards but rather are motivated by an individualized vision for success.

In place of expecting results according to narrow academic standards, we should instead define measurable goals and benchmarks for each school to reach annually as part of a larger, individual timeline. Success in public education means taking every student to the highest level that he or she can reach, whether that is pursuing an associate degree before moving on to a four-year degree program, a technical certification, or an advanced professional degree. By focusing on individual students and benchmarks in areas such as reading comprehension, fundamental math skills, critical thinking, high school graduation, and adequately preparing for a career or higher education, we will achieve a much more significant return for on investment in public education.

In our current education system, we rarely pay attention to individual student performance outside of averages. The fundamental flaw in the way that schools are evaluated is partly that—considering total public school enrollment exceeds 1.7 million students—averages can be extraordinarily misleading and often skew results to hide deficiencies. The average of 11 and 9 is 10—but so is the average of 1 and 19.

The most important attribute in a successful workforce is education and training because it gives people the ability to take advantage of growth in our economy so they can move into better jobs when they are created. It doesn't matter what or how many jobs are available if our workforce doesn't have the ability to perform their requirements.

While much of Georgia has experienced substantial economic development in recent decades, some of our rural counties have not been afforded the same opportunities to grow, which many of our state's suburban communities are capitalizing on.[101] Conversely, many of our state's urban schools have faced different challenges that are as equally daunting. It has been proven that if any city or county has a sub-standard public education system, over time it will be difficult to avoid economic decline, and that community will be more likely to lose population than sustain growth. *If we were able to regain that lost opportunity through an improved public education system, what would Georgia look like? How much better off would all of our citizens be?*

One extreme example of lost potential that our state must move past is the Atlanta Public Schools cheating scandal. On April 1, 2015, eleven former Atlanta Public Schools educators were convicted in the largest standardized test cheating scandal in American history.[102] A state investigation conducted in 2010 found evidence of cheating in 44 out of 56 schools in Atlanta's system of more than 48,000 students.[103] Thirty-five teachers, principals, and administrators were ultimately indicted as part of the investigation.[104] We may never know the depth of the wrongdoing, but prosecutors argued that APS teachers, principals, and administrators erased incorrect answers on standardized tests, and, in some cases, instructed students to change their answers in order to receive promotions and cash bonuses during the 2009 school year.

The Atlanta Public Schools scandal should have never happened. In the end, there were no winners and thousands of students were seriously setback academically. To their credit, Atlanta Public Schools have since committed to becoming a charter system and holistically reforming operations.[105] I am hopeful that with strong leadership, good teachers and principals and community support, APS will grow to represent a positive example of the transformative innovations that are now possible in public education.

In addition to challenging America to send a man to the moon, President John F. Kennedy also popularized the saying "a rising tide lifts all boats." [106] There is no better analogy for what will happen when we invigorate economic growth in every single community across Georgia. Furthermore, we will achieve state-wide success after we give every high school student access to a College and Career Academy and the option of graduating from high school with an associate degree or earning a technical certification to pursue a rewarding career in one of our state's advanced industries.

The core pillar of any business plan is to find a need and meet the challenge of satisfying consumer demand. Many of the issues facing rural and urban schools alike involve a pattern of decline that is decades in the making. If we are serious about reversing this trend, restructuring public education must be our highest priority. This shift is critical. When a community is facing longstanding inequalities—poverty, crime, stalling economic development, declining populations and available resources—deficiencies in that community's public schools are amplified through nearly every area of consequence. Fortunately, the reverse can also become true. We can drive generational change from inside of our public schools. When we direct our focus to improving public education, our communities become capable of removing the barriers which constrain our success and growth as a society. The same mindset that has allowed technology to revolutionize our lives should be applied to public education reform. Fortunately, with modern technology, schools have the ability to track individual student performance in extraordinary detail from enrollment until graduation. With this advantage and safeguards to ensure accountability from school-level leaders, we have the ability to completely redesign our public education system from the ground up. Our reward will be measured by individual student outcomes and is limitless in its potential to catalyze something greater. Through shifting our focus, we will also improve our understanding of the factors that cause widespread differences in academic performance between and within our state's schools.

8

What's New? Moving all of Georgia's Students Forward

I like the dreams of the future better than the history of the past.[107]
—Thomas Jefferson

My vision to comprehensively redesign the way in which Georgia's public schools educate our students is founded upon the idea that the only way we will accomplish our mission is by encouraging each school to embrace its individuality, and to adopt a strategy that addresses the specific challenges its students are facing. The most fundamental decisions schools make are with respect to structuring their management and administrative operations, and determining which teachers and faculty to hire, retain, and promote. Rather than encouraging all schools to conform to any statewide status quo, local leaders should be empowered with the right to determine the governance and employment practices of their schools.

We should recognize that there is no one model or classroom curricula that any school will be able to rely upon in perpetuity or that can satisfy what students will need to learn for a length of time greater than a single school year. Safeguards are essential, and it isn't difficult for the state of Georgia to ascribe basic parameters for different grade levels without micromanaging each school's operations.

Today, thousands of teachers make an effort to incorporate real-world demonstrations into lesson plans to help students understand how the concepts they are learning apply to their lives. However, in no way does our public education system provide teachers the incentive to put forward the extra effort required to integrate more active learning curriculum into their classrooms. All things considered, we do more to hold teachers back from doing something that may be controversial than to encourage them to change students' lives for the better. If a student becomes disengaged and falls behind academically, the presence of relatable applications to the concepts they are learning—in addition to good teachers—can make the difference between dropping out and graduating. Too many teachers are spending significant portions of their days addressing disciplinary problems. We need a cultural change across our public education system to reset our priorities in favor of addressing individual problems early and honestly—and giving all students every opportunity to learn.

We have to allow all of our schools to innovate so they can find new ways of accomplishing individualized objectives every day. We also shouldn't be afraid to give students and parents choices to determine the paths that will shape the direction of their futures. Above all, we need strong leaders at every level of our public education system who refuse to settle for anything less than another opportunity to improve and relentlessly strive for new heights in academic performance.

RESPONDING TO THE CHALLENGE
OF A GENERATION

In government, change is usually the exception and because of how difficult it is to challenge the status quo in public education, it can sometimes appear as though we are willing to accept that a certain number of people will fall through the cracks for the sake of achieving a system-wide average. In the long term, however, it will no longer be possible to value the education of one student more than another because to do so is to deny that America was built upon the premise that no matter who your parents are, and no matter the circumstances under which you were born, every person is entitled to earn whatever his or her abilities can afford them. No authority is entitled to say that achieving anything is impossible for anyone. When we stop aspiring to do better as a society in pursuit of this ideal, we will lose the spirit that makes America exceptional. In combination with our nation's free market economy, public education will always be the great equalizer in our society.

The truth is that no one really knows how well public schools are educating Georgia's students except for the teachers in each classroom. Statewide, we still don't recognize in a meaningful way what individual students achieve from year-to-year throughout most of their education. The challenge we face is that school systems are not developing proactive programs to prevent students from falling through the cracks. That is, we aren't doing enough for students before they move toward graduating from high school—or drop out—and try to realize their dreams. At that point if their educations are subpar, these individuals will join hundreds of thousands of people in our state and find themselves unemployed or unable to retain employment because they are not in possession of in-demand skills.

More people are graduating from high school with limited skills but fewer jobs are being created that will hire individuals with a conventional high school diploma and no additional training. This negative employment trend has amplified a larger challenge, which we must also confront because the value of a high school diploma is no longer adequate in our economy. On far too many occasions, when discussing how to increase graduation rates in our high schools, I have been offered suggestions of ways in which we may be able to further devalue the diplomas our students earn. Suggestions like reducing the rigor of courses required, decreasing expectations for student achievement or finding creative excuses for social promotion. I reject this way of thinking about how we educate our students. Solutions will be found through innovations developed in schools that ask questions like: *How can we add value to the degrees our students receive? What can we do to think long-term about the skills our graduates require to be successful in an ever-changing economy? Which alternatives can we offer students so that no one will give into the temptation of dropping out to secure a shortsighted monetary benefit?* For too many students, the decision to drop out of school is easy. Recognizing this reality, our schools must innovate to add value to their education with practical programs that can make meaningful impacts in the lives of all students.

In conjunction with public schools in each community, College and Career Academies can support retraining and work certification programs. In fact, each College and Career Academy is free to coordinate specific training programs with individual companies under its own mutually agreed upon terms. By building College and Career Academies to serve every single high school student in Georgia by 2020, we can take a big step toward offering everyone a renewed opportunity to gain the skills and certifications necessary to get a job in one of Georgia's high-demand trades or growing industries.

For most of my adult life, the successes and failures of our public education system have felt personal to me. As a policymaker who has been involved in legislative efforts on public education issues, I can say with some authority that, despite our best efforts, we haven't been successful in adapting our public schools to meet the real-time demands of people across our state. Just as importantly, in the near term, we aren't preparing our students to compete globally at the level demanded in the twenty-first century. We can determine that we haven't done enough to encourage innovation in public education because most of our schools continue to resist implementing major changes in how students are being taught.

So, what needs to happen in order for every school to innovate in its own right? Even in the case of the two most significant legislative reform efforts I've led in public education—creating charter systems and College and Career Academies—I have been disappointed by how few schools have taken advantage of their new-found freedom and flexibility. It has been equally frustrating to see that many schools have attempted to adopt these measures, in large part, by name only. A number of school systems are seeking to implement only the better-vetted reforms, avoiding anything that might be criticized or viewed as risky. Leaders in these systems seem content to settle with the moderate level of improvement in student performance, which is likely to arise from shifting basic decision-making authority to local control.

It is very difficult to make comprehensive reform a reality in public schools, but we don't have a choice of whether or not to try to the best of our ability. In some cases, the most logical conclusion I can draw is that these schools are waiting for a bolder, better-positioned school to do the heavy lifting and take the risk of innovating. At that point, after someone else develops new academic programs and class structures that are more effective, everyone else can adopt them too. Unfortunately that is not how innovation works and it will not lead to long-term success for the students enrolled in schools that adopt this approach. This is not a choice; we must demand a cultural change in all of our public schools.

When it comes to administering some of our government's most critical programs, our elected leaders have an unfortunate tendency to set lofty objectives that, as time passes, only superficially meet their goals. Under decades-old programs such as these, if and when major impediments arise to prevent the objectives from being fully achieved, we perplexingly tend to ignore our most serious problems and hope to succeed in spite of them.

In public education, we have tried to implement a number of solutions that sidestep our statewide system's most serious structural flaws and instead attempt to make the symptoms less severe. This is the true of academic achievement and the widespread use of standardized tests to measure the performance of students, and to compare averages across different schools. In this case, government intervention has artificially created deficiencies in the academic performance of millions of students nationwide while ignoring most other assessments of individual performance taken throughout the regular school year.

The time has come for the federal government to back off its interventionist role in public education and to fully restore governance authority to the states. The alternative—accepting the use of state-to-state standardized test score comparisons—is a false choice because it exists only at the expense of our students' academic interests.

After twelve years of using the CRCT to evaluate student performance, a broad consensus of education professionals determined that our state's use of the standardized test was hurting our students.[108] In the 2014 school year, the Georgia Milestones Assessment System was introduced to replace the CRCT as our state's official standardized test.[109] I am not willing to wait another decade or more to learn that our students still aren't where we want them to be academically because schools have wasted more time and resources training students to score well on a new standardized test. There is nothing wrong with testing our students for basic comprehension but the stakes that we set must reflect the reliability of the methods we are using to evaluate students. In the case of standardized testing this too is best calibrated at the school level as part of individualized learning plans.

Although it is frustrating to see how slowly change moves, we must continue to demand transformational innovation from every single school. In recent years, we have made significant progress and the infrastructure being developed by charter systems and College and Career Academies will undoubtedly be a valuable asset as we move toward embracing new, systematic reforms. Creating the right infrastructure within any organization is critical so that leaders at each level can work both individually and in unison to achieve our broader goals. Schools cannot succeed without effective leadership from teachers, administrators, and principals, and the state of Georgia cannot move forward as a whole without a clear vision for our future and leadership dedicated to maintaining the quality of life we all hope to have.

The same attributes that will make a state senator an ineffective representative of his or her constituents can also describe a complacent local school board member or superintendent. We elect our neighbors to represent us in public offices because we trust them to carry out the promises they make and to be honest and trustworthy stewards of government. In public service, leadership means not shying away from confrontation and making forward-looking decisions with integrity. In public forums, local school board members should ask their constituents: *What are the specific problems facing each of our schools?* Then with principals, teachers, parents, and their communities, they must determine the best path forward.

It is my responsibility to encourage individuals who are able and willing to help improve our communities to run for public office, especially for our state's local school boards. The Office of Lieutenant Governor belongs to the people of Georgia. I have never viewed any public office as something that was mine to lose in the next election but, sadly, across our nation a number of representatives do.

Today, however, I am more optimistic than I have ever been about Georgia's ability to capitalize on our potential and assert our state as a global economic leader. I have confidence in our ability to meet the challenge of building a world-class system of public education because the vast majority of people in our state are fully aware of both our shortfalls and the degree to which we could all do better. Equally, the public and private sectors are recognizing that we can't afford to wait any longer to address our longstanding challenges in public education.

There are better ways to educate students but there is no one way that will work for every school system or even in the majority of classrooms. True reform will require decisive leadership and years of making difficult choices. It will be jarring to many people to realize the full extent of what it takes to build a world-class public education system but it is worth taking on the greatest challenge of our generation and making public education our highest priority in order to secure a prosperous future for our kids.

THE DIFFERENCE BETWEEN SUCCESS AND FAILURE: WHAT DO WE HAVE TO LOSE?

For most people, it's difficult to make major changes to how they lead their day-to-day lives. One of the most common reasons people resist change is because it means stepping outside of their comfort zones and facing harsh realities if they want to pursue something better. Instead of fighting complacency, it seems easier to skip ahead and acknowledge that we'll have to settle at some point so we can set "realistic" expectations. In public education, conventional wisdom dictates that we should be content with marginal improvements in standardized test score averages each year and that there is a formula for these tests to work well enough that they will continue to be our most useful tools in measuring academic performance.

The absence of innovation in public education has created a void that private companies are starting to fill. Many consumers of our public education system—both parents and students—are, to varying degrees, opting out and seeking private academic support. More parents are paying to enroll their kids in supplemental programs that focus on strengthening their academic abilities in core areas such as reading and writing comprehension, math and science, and vocational learning. Online companies are also taking over where our public schools are falling short. In recent years, technology has facilitated the growth of a K–12 education marketplace expansion that now extends far beyond traditional outside alternatives such as private schools and tutors.

One of the leading startups increasing access to online academic resources is the Khan Academy. Today, the Khan Academy provides free academic practice exercises, instructional videos, and individualized learning profiles to more than 28 million users globally.[110] Though he didn't have a background working in education, founder Sal Khan is an MIT graduate (with three degrees) who earned an MBA from Harvard and describes himself as being passionate about mathematics.[111]

On a 2004 visit to New Orleans, Khan discovered that his cousin Nadia was struggling in math and would be moved to a less rigorous class the following school year.[112] To Khan, this wasn't acceptable. He knew how important it would become to keep Nadia from falling further behind in math so he offered to help. Because Khan lived in Boston, he started tutoring Nadia by phone. After he helped Nadia improve her performance in math, Khan started accepting additional requests from family members to tutor them as well. Soon, it became overwhelming to balance his job as a financial analyst with offering multiple tutoring sessions each week. To streamline his efforts, Khan followed what sounded like a novel suggestion at the time and began posting his tutorials on YouTube.

Until 2009, Khan balanced his work in finance with recording tutorial videos when he had spare time. But after taking notice of how popular his tutorials had become, Khan left his job and started working full time to develop the Khan Academy. In 2010, the Bill and Melinda Gates Foundation granted the Khan Academy seed funding.[113] Shortly thereafter, Google and several other investors made similarly sizable contributions to help advance Khan's mission of giving everyone with Internet access the academic resources needed to learn by themselves. With a comprehensive set of tutorials that range from primary to collegiate levels—all centrally available on the Khan Academy's learning platform—millions of students have gained a new opportunity to understand advanced concepts at their own pace.

The Khan Academy's videos cover everything from basic arithmetic all the way through college level math, science, and economics. The website's learning profiles also monitor user activity to identify each student's strengths and weaknesses, while allowing users to review information for as long as necessary. Because of YouTube, the Khan Academy has grown into an entity that offers quality tutorials in a wide array of subjects at no cost to users, and can be accessed by anyone with an Internet connection. Technology has significantly reduced the cost of introducing new innovations such as the Khan Academy into the marketplace.

Because of the growing perception that our public schools are failing, several private companies, including Connections Academy, Edison Learning, and K–12, are also developing alternatives to traditional public schools.[114] These companies facilitate the operations of state charter schools that use an online platform to match students with individualized learning plans. The Georgia Department of Education's program, Georgia Virtual School, provides similar options to students in school districts throughout our state.[115] Though the merit of enrolling in private online programs as an alternative to attending a traditional public school is unproven, these schools clearly demonstrate that the technology to design individualized learning plans at the classroom level does, in fact, exist.

Some charter systems have started developing their own online instructional programming. For example, the Calhoun City Charter System launched an online academy where students are offered expanded course offerings and flexible enrollment options.[116] This is one program helping to address a major shortfall in our public schools, whereby we have a tendency to rush students through each grade level and punish those who don't learn with poor grades. In the process of doing so, we set these students up to fail by expecting they will learn more complex information in the next grade level despite their failure to grasp the prerequisite concepts they needed to learn in previous years. I understand why it makes sense for some families to choose to enroll their kids in virtual public schools; however, we cannot expect to become successful in public education reform by simply outsourcing the functions of traditional public schools online.

I believe that the state of Georgia has approximately five years to reform our public education system. If we do not shift our focus to achieving better outcomes for students, then our economy will sustain permanent structural declines in employment. A predictable divide is already growing between students, in terms of prospective educational outcomes, based on circumstances outside their individual control. This divide will only get larger. Poverty will increase and if we fail to give Georgians hope, criminal activity may become a more tempting alternative. Worst of all, if we reach a point of no return, we will have no choice but to standby and watch our families, communities, and economy suffer further under the pressures of decline. Thus, it is incumbent upon each of us to ensure that every Georgian has the types of opportunities that I was given to earn a better life.

Maybe repeated failures to reform the way that our public schools operate has contributed to a growing cynicism, rooted in the public's perception that our government has little ability to keep promises or do anything that will improve our lives. Perhaps the pressure of self-fulfilling predictions that our schools will fail no matter what we do has caused so many of our schools to adopt a play-it-safe approach, feeling more comfortable as part of the status quo. In any case, if we do not transform the way in which our students are being educated, we will lose the positive momentum our state has experienced. If we do not demand better public schools, our society will accelerate towards a decline. Continuing to ignore our obligation to prepare Georgia's students to be successful in the twenty-first century will ensure that our children inherit a future in which our society grows more divided.

9

Beyond Potential—
Achieving Positive Educational Outcomes

The philosophy of the school room in one generation will be the philosophy of government in the next.[117]

—Abraham Lincoln

We have a responsibility to reform our public education system to ensure that when all of our schools are successful absolutely no students will drop out of high school. To sincerely begin the process of reform, every school in Georgia must affirm its commitment to not allowing even a single student to fall behind academically and have his or her deficiencies ignored. Our schools have to go further than just the appearance of a 100 percent graduation rate; we must demand that every single student graduate from high school with the knowledge, skills, and experience needed to be either college or career ready. Our obligation to expect 100 percent of our students to graduate—and for every high school diploma to have real marketable value—arises from the fact that as we move further into the twenty-first century, the quality of the educations that our children receive will be increasingly determinative of their ability to realize success and significance later in life.

Although we all have different definitions of success and significance, we can, nonetheless describe a distinct and essential set of outcomes. Success is based entirely on personal achievement, and as such, can be measured professionally, monetarily, or with respect to another pursuit that an individual holds value in attaining or living in accordance with. On the other hand, leading a life of significance requires someone to have a meaningful role in the lives of others. Undoubtedly, an individual who is employed with a rewarding career will gain happiness by advancing professionally and accumulating material wealth. But raising our kids to be productive and personally successful people, providing for our families, and, more generally, being a part of something bigger than ourselves, will lead most people to experience the more fulfilling reward that is personal significance.

The only way for our public schools to ensure that every single student can succeed academically and personally is by wholly abandoning the myriad of top-down mandates and regulations that have permitted thousands of students to fall through the cracks and fail out of school. Regardless of how well thought out any proposals to improve public education may appear, nothing will change unless teachers are given greater authority to make meaningful decisions that serve in the best interest of their students. Using formative assessments to replace the high-stakes summative assessments that we are currently using will provide the necessary link of accountability to empower all of our teachers with greater decision-making authority in their classrooms.

Generally, I think that government programs serve our citizens most effectively when following a defined plan of action that is designed to achieve specific and measurable objectives. By analyzing the challenges that confront different public schools across the state of Georgia, if nothing else, I have learned that a statewide one-size-fits-all system will never generate the outcomes that our students deserve. It is simply impossible to claim that if a student follows a pre-determined course of learning or scores well on a standardized test, that individual will achieve a specific educational outcome, professionally or otherwise.

Schools cannot succeed without effective leadership from principals, administrators, and teachers. Alternatively, they will also benefit from targeted support from their locally elected school boards and the superintendents whom they appoint. On a larger level, just as local schools cannot excel without developing new strategic plans, the state of Georgia cannot move forward without a clear vision for our future. Our success depends on having statewide leadership dedicated to achieving the future we all hope to live. A rising tide lifts all boats, and excellence in public education will drive prosperity in all our communities.

THE ROAD AHEAD

Repeatedly, I have asked: *With respect to the outcome for individual students, what is the purpose of public education?* I believe that the purpose of our public education system is to prepare every single person educated in the state of Georgia to be either college-bound, after earning an associate degree whenever possible, or career-ready immediately after graduating from high school. In this chapter, I will offer as thorough of an answer as possible to the question of what our children should expect from each of their schools. In doing so, I will outline three core benchmarks that will transform the way in which Georgia approaches public education, and in turn, unleash the potential of everyone in our state to excel academically and professionally.

By creating charter systems, we have already empowered our state's public schools to adopt accountability contracts as a mechanism of shifting decision-making and instructional programming authority as close to students, teachers, principals, and school-level leaders as possible. Simply described, accountability contracts are individualized, objectives-based agreements, under which school districts outline a strategic plan to offer students high quality educations.

The first benchmark of education reform is for all of Georgia's school districts to commit to meeting a defined set of goals

that will improve the academic performance of their students under a five year strategic plan, using accountability contracts to empower teachers, principals, and school-level leaders with decision-making authority. In addition to giving teachers and each school's leadership ownership over our students' educations by providing them with meaningful management and instructional authority, accountability contracts establish parameters to hold teachers, principals, and local governance leaders accountable for reaching detailed objectives. By clearly defining an overarching performance strategy for the next school year based on factors specific to individual districts and schools, accountability contracts help to unite principals, administrators, teachers, and faculty to work together for their students.

There is no such thing as a standardized contract because precise terms are required to generate specific outcomes from any contract, whether in business or education. But by recognizing the challenges faced by each school system with an individualized accountability contract in districts statewide, we can set achievable goals to put all of our schools on the best possible path for students to achieve educational excellence. Once in place, accountability contracts will also allow primary and secondary schools to divide their operations more effectively.

For our schools to be successful, it takes more than just great principals or well-intentioned teachers. Every single member of each school's faculty must contribute as part of a governance team, which should also include other valuable members of each community who can contribute expertise or resources. Local leadership and school-level decision-making are the best ways to unleash our students, parents, business leaders, and communities as a whole to move forward together.

We will achieve the second benchmark of public education reform when Georgia's schools effectively create individualized

learning plans to track each student's academic performance. Our state's elementary and middle schools should direct their focus on providing students with a foundational base of knowledge in each core academic subject. Then, high schools must effectively prepare all of our students to graduate with the skills and experience necessary to advance in college, or to be immediately employable.

Technology has introduced new ways to teach, learn, evaluate, and record academic performance that should give us confidence in the ability of our schools to take ownership over decision-making in return for accepting accountability over the results. Using formative assessments to measure academic performance, and individualized learning plans that follow students from enrollment until they earn a high school diploma, we can gain an unprecedented view into how our schools are educating students.

We have long known that each school can implement decisions for its students better than the most effective national or statewide system, but we finally have the tools to verify it. Now, all we have to do is allow public schools to innovate. Using individualized learning plans, our state's primary schools should shift their focus to ensuring that all of our students are proficient in the core academic subjects—including reading and writing, mathematics, science, and social studies—before graduating them from the eighth grade. Electronically streamlining individualized learning plans with academic records will improve the effectiveness, efficiency, and transparency of each school's operations.

Part of the reason individualized learning plans are so important is because they are an acknowledgement that our students have to continue learning and gaining new skills and experience. Henry Ford once said: "Anyone who stops learning is old, whether at twenty or eighty. Anyone who keeps learning stays young."[118] In my own life, I have observed this philosophy to be true.

Before my mom and step-dad took out a second mortgage on their house to help me buy my first business, I made a promise to my mom. Although we both knew that I wouldn't be able to continue taking morning and night classes at Gainesville College because I had to devote all of my attention to making my business successful, I promised my mom that I would finish college and earn my degree. To honor that commitment, during my first term as lieutenant governor, I made the decision to enroll in a program to finish my associate degree at Brenau University. When I completed the program and graduated, it was personally satisfying to know that I had fulfilled an important promise. But to an equally great effect, completing my education enriched my life and helped me to realize how rewarding it can be to take advantage of every day as a new opportunity to learn.

The third benchmark of my vision for comprehensive public education reform is to permanently change the structure of every high school in the state of Georgia. In chapter six, "Why Industry Matters," I introduced the concept of College and Career Academies and declared my commitment to making sure every student in our state has access to a College and Career Academy by 2020. Ultimately, all of our state's students should divide their four years of high school between two years of core academic and elective classes, and two years at a College and Career Academy, during which time they either prepare to obtain a four-year college degree and earn an associate degree, or enroll in a certification program to train for a career.

Too many college students are enrolling in remedial classes to supplement academic deficiencies in subjects such as math and writing. An even larger number of students are moving to campuses at colleges and universities across our state without any idea of what they want to study or achieve professionally. Many of our students intuitively seek more freedom in high school. We should use our high schools to take advantage of students' desire to learn, and expand their campuses by making College and Career Academies available to every single student. Doing so will allow all of our students to determine what they are passionate about in the eleventh and twelfth grades, and to decide what path to pursue after high school before they are forced to confront an ultimatum of whether or not to attend a four-year college.

In my role as lieutenant governor, I have made hundreds of visits to rural communities across Georgia. I regularly meet with residents, business leaders, and local officials from cities and counties all over our state. On several occasions, in meetings with large employers considering expansion sites that would create new jobs in Georgia, CEO's have told me directly that they don't believe it is possible to find the workforce they need in many of our rural communities. Some companies have started to factor in the cost of hiring applicants from out of state because they have calculated that to be the easiest way to find people who are able to fill the jobs their businesses will create in engineering, technology, and healthcare. Businesses have discovered that individuals, who have families, and are qualified for high-demand careers, will refuse to move to a community with poorly performing public schools. In this respect, a single community's education system not only impacts that individual city or county, which alone may have tens of thousands of kids, but also has significant and long-term implications for our statewide economic network.

We do not live in an ideal world where our public schools can be seamlessly aligned with 100 percent of real demands for professions that exist in our economy. We should at least acknowledge that almost everyone will join the job market at some point after graduating from high school or college. Preparing all of our students to be college or career ready is important for the success of our economy, but it is even more critical for the livelihood of millions of people in communities throughout Georgia. People have to be able to earn a livable wage to survive, and if our cities and counties—especially those in rural Georgia—are not growing, they are more than likely in decline.

In the absence of a clear mission for our public education system, the concepts of accountability contracts and individualized learning plans, which are critical to my vision for the future of our public schools, don't have meaning. If every school began to implement individualized learning plans tomorrow—without a cohesive mission—the majority of students would benefit only marginally, if at all. Despite what many of us would wish, there isn't one simple answer that will work for every student. Instead, the solution is to meet students where they are, chart an individualized course, and empower our teachers to lead each student to become successful.

Georgia is always at its best when we are stretching to achieve something better. The only choice that we should never consider is whether to settle for anything less than a better future for our kids. We cannot afford to stop improving, and our public schools have to keep innovating. There is no such thing as a perfect education, and I can predict with confidence that no such ideal will ever exist. However, that is exactly why we shouldn't be afraid to fail. If we allow each of our public schools to put forward its best effort, we can only improve. Although some of our leaders may fear the unknown, our children—the students who are being educated in our schools—can never be asked to choose whether to confront the long-term consequences of inadequacies in the value of the educations being delivered by our public schools.

10

Conclusion

There are no great limits to growth because there are no limits of human intelligence, imagination, and wonder.[119]

—Ronald Reagan

Most people agree that we need to comprehensively reform public education to refocus attention on our students to the greatest extent possible. There have been calls for decades to fundamentally change the way in which our nation's schools educate our children. But even as we have dedicated more money to funding new programs, moved towards measuring student performance with different standardized tests, and implemented a multitude of top-down mandates, concerns across the country about the future of public schools have only become more pressing, and calls for change from students, parents, and business leaders have rightfully grown louder. We must work to give every school in the state of Georgia the tools to move forward on a defined five year path of reform, in which teachers, principals, and local leaders are individually empowered to redefine what it means to provide an education to students in exchange for taking accountability over the results and reaching determined performance objectives.

I understand exactly how formidable the challenge of reforming public education is, but I also know that charter systems and College and Career Academies are proving every day that we can redesign our schools to provide high quality educations to all our students. When we unleash the potential of communities to contribute to the success of public schools, I am confident in the ability of people across our state to come together and move forward by implementing real, long-term solutions. We will be successful, and by improving the quality of our public education system, we will make an investment that offers an incredibly significant return, improving the quality of life throughout our state. We can build a public education system that sets a clear academic floor with no cracks that also has no ceiling and advances all of our students as far as their individual abilities will take them.

All of our principals have to be excellent, and all of our teachers have to be exceptional. Excellent principals select, retain, and promote quality teachers, provide instructional leadership, ensure that schools are safe and operating efficiently, and bring together the components necessary to deliver a balanced education to students. Exceptional teachers work to give students every opportunity to learn, investing in them personally by putting forward time and effort to match the way each individual learns with the knowledge and skills that he or she needs to become academically proficient in any given subject. Teachers and principals—supported by administrators, counselors, and staff members—are our most powerful resources. We should take advantage of using individualized learning plans and employing a wide range of academic performance indicators that can be collected at any given time to monitor each student's performance, especially in elementary and middle schools.

Charter systems provide the model for an accountability contract that demonstrates how to make our schools conduits for external resources by incorporating parents, local businesses, and service organizations into the educational process. It may be that access to a local mentoring program will help students who struggle with personal issues become successful in school. Or that Usher's New Look Foundation may be able to help groups of students from different schools improve their academic performance by participating in an extracurricular leadership program. Incorporating all of these dimensions will improve the ability of Georgia's schools to provide instructional pathways for students from the time they enroll in public schools—typically around age five—until they graduate approximately thirteen years later. Each student would receive an education that allows him or her to pursue the same diversity of opportunity reflected in our economy.

Empowering public schools to exercise local management by entering into an individualized accountability contract is one of the core policy reforms that will transform public education in our state. We can never forget that the end goal of K–12 education is to provide every single person with an opportunity to obtain the knowledge, skills, and experience necessary to move forward and realize personal, academic, and professional success in their lives after graduating from high school.

We have to adopt a new mindset that rewards innovation rather than compliance with mandates so that we can empower our teachers and principals with significant decision-making authority. Part of our path to establishing Georgia's public schools as models of innovation and academic success is to provide every single high school student with access to a College and Career Academy. We also must continue expanding our network of charter systems to include more districts that are prepared to take advantage of the benefits. All of our districts should work with schools to establish individual measures of accountability for teachers and principals to meet in exchange for being granted greater decision-making authority. Ultimately, the most important metric of our success will be the progress that we make towards graduating 100 percent of the students who enroll in Georgia's public schools, while ensuring they possess the knowledge and skills necessary to be fully prepared for any academic program in college—earning an associate degree whenever possible—or trained and employable for a high-demand career after graduating from high school.

If we start with the right outlook, immediately, we can move past the superficial debates that have polluted our education system with countless rules and regulations that are impossible to implement. The American Dream is very much alive, and entrepreneurship still works. When we stop talking about doing the minimum—as we do when we discuss statewide standards or Common Core—we can move forward and start building a new public education system based entirely on what we know is required for individuals to become successful in the twenty-first century.

I do not advocate lowering Georgia's expectations for our public schools in any way. It is imperative for our state government to apply a fair process of evaluation to individual school systems that allows them to innovate and accomplish objectives as effectively as possible. But our focus should always rest on students and within communities. Strengthening public schools will improve local economies, and if given the opportunity, I am confident that many of Georgia's businesses and community leaders will join us and invest in educational programs that benefit all our residents.

As Georgia's lieutenant governor, I believe that I have an obligation to do everything in my power to improve our state's schools so we can honestly say to all of our students, without exception, that their educations are of a high enough quality to enable them to be successful in any academic or professional endeavor they choose to pursue. Public education is the core function of government that provides the foundational promise of opportunity to Georgia's citizens and represents our collective hope for the future, which will always be represented by our state's children. The only way that we can unleash the potential of our students is with leadership from school-level decision makers.

Providing the education that all of our students require and deserve is not a short-term policy goal, but, instead, depends on fulfilling a commitment to making continual statewide progress as we work to increase student access to resources and educational pathways, and grant ownership to more teachers, principals, and school-level leaders with accountability contracts. We also have to encourage local innovation and shared community economic development, centered around College and Career Academies. Lasting education reform will change the way in which students prepare for and complete post-secondary levels of education. As we create system-wide change, the impact will be felt by students, teachers, principals, school leaders and faculty, communities, and statewide economic development. These are the areas of reform that will expand and develop to make the state of Georgia successful in the future.

We will succeed by following the guiding principals that we know are critical, and above all, never losing focus from the academic performance of individual students. Our schools should all strive to create and implement strategic plans that will promote an environment of academic quality, specialization of learning and skill training, and excellence through achievement. By reforming our public education system and adjusting our mindsets to demonstrate that the educations our children receive should be at the core of our families, communities, and—without a doubt—be the focus in every single one of our schools, we will grow together to become a stronger and more united Georgia.

Changing the culture of our schools, and redesigning the way in which we educate students, will require collaborative input from all of the stakeholders who want to share in the benefits of economic growth in Georgia's future. No one can stay on the sidelines. Students, parents, teachers, and business leaders have to join together to create new initiatives and instructional programs that enable all of our students to realize academic success and achieve personal significance. If we are going to elevate our public education system to reach the quality that we want for our students, we cannot afford to leave any resources on the table. This means asking individually: *What can I do to help improve my community's public schools?* Georgia's moment is now. I know that we will rise to meet all of the challenges we face along the way to reaching our destiny. Our first step is to guarantee that education is unleashed.

End Notes

[1] http://kingencyclopedia.stanford.edu/encyclopedia/documentsentry/doc_470200_000/.

[2] http://www.un.org/en/globalissues/briefingpapers/efa/quotes.shtml.

[3] https://www.gadoe.org/External-Affairs-and-Policy/AskDOE/Pages/Schools-and-Districts.aspx.

[4] http://dailyedventures.com/index.php/2012/11/08/michael-horn/.

[5] http://ccrpi.gadoe.org.

[6] http://ccrpi.gadoe.org/2014/ccrpi2014.aspx.

[7] http://www.gadoe.org/External-Affairs-and-Policy/State-Board-of-Education/SBOE%20Rules/160-4-9-.04.pdf.

[8] http://www.dublinschools.net/protected/ArticleView.aspx?iid=5YIP3I&dasi=2G2

[9] http://georgiacareeracademies.org.

[10] http://www.gallup.com/businessjournal/505/Item-Companys-Mission-Purpose.aspx?g_source=VALUES&g_medium=topic&g_campaign=tiles.

[11] http://www.forbes.com/sites/lewishowes/2012/07/17/20-business-quotes-and-lessons-from-walt-disney/.

[12] http://www.brookings.edu/~/media/research/files/reports/2011/10/27-state-budgets-gordon/1027_state_budgets_gordon.pdf.

[13] http://media.ethics.ga.gov/search/campaign/Campaign_Name.aspx?NameID=315&FilerID=C2006000098&Type=candidate.

[14] http://dlg.galileo.usg.edu/cgi-bin/govdimag.cgi?path=dbs/1994/ga/s700/_ps1/s4/1994/folio.con/&user=galileo&sessionid=43bfd109-1456810429-1481&serverid=DU&instcode=PUBL&return=ggpd%3fuserid%3dgalileo%26dbs%3dggpd%26action%3dretrieve%26recno%3d1%26numrecs%3d25%26__rtype%3drecno%26key%3dy-ga-bs700-b-ps1-bs4-b1994-bfolio.

[15] http://www.senate.ga.gov/senators/en-US/SenateMembersList.aspx

[16] http://media.ethics.ga.gov/search/campaign/CCDR_Report_Summary.aspx?NameID=451&FilerID=C2006000159&CDRID=3339&Name=Reed%20Jr.,%20Ralph%20E.&Year=2006&Report=June%2030th%20-%20Election%20Year.

[17] http://www.tiftongazette.com/news/local_news/cagle-stumps-in-tifton/article_94886c00-d4a7-5d17-b24a-f3b39777e85f.html; http://www.gainesvilletimes.com/archives/2319/.

[18] Joseph Demakis, *The Ultimate Book of Quotations* (Raleigh, NC: Lulu Enterprises, 2012).

[19] http://www.senate.ga.gov/Documents/gaconstitution.pdf.

[20] http://gbpi.org/wp-content/uploads/2014/01/Overview-2015-K-12.pdf.

[21] https://federaleducationpolicy.wordpress.com/2011/02/19/1867-act-to-establish-a-federal-department-of-education/.

[22] http://www2.ed.gov/about/overview/focus/what_pg2.html.

[23] Bonnie Beyer and Eileen S. Johnson, *Special Programs and Services in Schools: Creating Options, Meeting Needs* (Lancaster, PA: DEStech Publications, 2014).

[24] Jimmy Carter, "Department of Education Organization Act Statement on Signing S. 210 Into Law," 17 October 1979, online by Gerhard Peters and John T. Woolley, *The American Presidency Project*, http://www.presidency.ucsb.edu/ws/?pid=31543.

[25] http://www.edweek.org/ew/section/multimedia/no-child-left-behind-overview-definition-summary.html.

[26] http://www.cmu.edu/teaching/assessment/howto/basics/formative-summative.html.

[27] http://www.house.ga.gov/budget/Documents/2016_FiscalYear/FY_2016_State_of_Georgia_Budget_Book.pdf.

[28] Richard Hyatt, *Zell: The Governor Who Gave Georgia HOPE, The Biography of Zell Miller* (Macon, GA: Mercer University Press, 1997).

[29] "High standards: More top students are staying home, pushing up admission criteria at Georgia colleges and universities," *Atlanta Business Chronicle*, 1 May 2015, http://www.bizjournals.com/atlanta/print-edition/2015/05/01/high-standards.html.

[30] http://webcache.googleusercontent.com/search?q=cache:YkxhtgA2LnwJ:www.gafcp.org/sys_gafcp/publications/BestPractices/causeshsdropout.doc+&cd=4&hl=en&ct=clnk&gl=us.

[31] http://www.legis.ga.gov/Legislation/Archives/19992000/leg/fulltext/sb67.htm.

[32] Georgia (State) Legislature, Senate Bill 36, *Quality Based Education Policies on Academic Performance for Promotion* 1999–2000 Reg. Sess. (3 March 1999) Georgia Senate, Cagle, Casey, http://www.legis.ga.gov/Legislation/Archives/19992000/leg/fulltext/sb36.htm.

[33] Georgia (State). Legislature, Senate Bill 69, *Education; enact the ABC Initiative; student assessment tests, reading program, grade placement committees* 2000–2001 Reg. Sess. (26 January 2001) Georgia Senate, Cagle, Casey, http://www.legis.ga.gov/Legislation/en-US/display/20012002/SB/69.

[34] http://www2.ed.gov/programs/racetothetop/index.html.

[35] https://ltgov.georgia.gov/charter-systems.

[36] https://www.gadoe.org/External-Affairs-and-Policy/Policy/Pages/IE2.aspx.

[37] https://app3.doe.k12.ga.us/ows-bin/owa/fte_pack_enrollgrade.entry_form.

[38] https://ltgov.georgia.gov/charter-systems.

[39] http://ltgov.georgia.gov/college-and-career-academies.

[40] http://www.nea.org/grants/55158.htm.

[41] https://app3.doe.k12.ga.us/ows-bin/owa/fte_pack_enroll grade.entry_form.

[42] https://www.gadoe.org/External-Affairs-and-Policy/AskDOE/Pages/Schools-and-Districts.aspx.

[43] http://hanushek.stanford.edu/publications/teacher-quality.

[44] Stephen Frank, Fuami Haastrup, and Ashley Woo. (2013) "ERS Policy Audit Report: An Examination of Georgia policies that affect the use of people, time, and money in Georgia's schools and districts."

[45] http://www.gadoe.org/Finance-and-Business-Operations/Budget-Services/Documents/FY15SalarySchedule_official.pdf.

[46] http://www.gadoe.org/Technology-Services/Data-Colletions/Documents/CPI%20Documentation/FY2016/State%20Salary%20Schedule.pdf.

[47] http://gbpi.org/wp-content/uploads/2014/01/Georgia-Budget-and-Policy-Institute-2015-Budget-Overview.pdf.

[48] https://hbr.org/2012/06/how-to-say-no-to-a-controlling.

[49] Georgia (State) Legislature, Senate Resolution 20, *Special Purpose County Sales Tax— use by local school system*1995–1996 Reg. Sess. (7 January 1995) Georgia Senate, Cagle, Casey, http://www.legis.ga.gov/Legislation/Archives/19951996/leg/fulltext/sr20.htm.

[50] http://www.senate.ga.gov/senators/en-US/SenateMembersList.aspx.

[51] Georgia (State) Legislature, Senate Resolution 125, *Special Purpose County Sales Tax—capital outlay projects for education* 1995–1996 Reg. Sess. (8 January 1995) Georgia Senate, Marable, Richard, http://www.legis.ga.gov/Legislation/Archives/19951996/leg/fulltext/sr125.htm.

[52] https://www.gadoe.org/Finance-and-Business-Operations/Facilities-Services/Pages/Splost.aspx.

[53] http://www.archives.gov/exhibits/charters/constitution.html.

[54] http://www.senate.ga.gov/Documents/gaconstitution.pdf.

[55] http://quickfacts.census.gov/qfd/states/13000.html

[56] https://ltgov.georgia.gov/charter-systems.

[57] http://www.gadoe.org/External-Affairs-and-Policy/Charter-Schools/Pages/General-Frequently-Asked-Questions.aspx.

[58] http://www.gadoe.org/External-Affairs-and-Policy/Charter-Schools/Pages/General-Frequently-Asked-Questions.aspx.

[59] https://gosa.georgia.gov/overview-gadoes-school-climate-star-rating.

[60] http://www.georgiatrend.com/August-2004/Friday-Night-Faithful/, GA Department of Audits and Accounts' Annual Report of School Salaries.

[61] http://www.marietta-city.org/cms/lib07/GA01903590/Centricity/Shared/files/Charter%20System/SGT%20Bylaws.pdf , http://www.marietta-city.org/Page/2350.

[62] http://www.gadoe.org/External-Affairs-and-Policy/Charter-Schools/Documents/2014%20Charter%20Schools%20and%20Charter%20Systems%20Annual%20Report%20-%20Rev%201%202015-01-14.pdf (Annual Report).

[63] Michael B. Becraft, *Bill Gates: A Biography* (Santa Barbara, CA: Greenwood, 2014).

[64] http://www.theguardian.com/small-business-network/2014/oct/28/top-reasons-small-businesses-fail.

[65] http://www.atlantafalcons.com/team/history.html, http://atlanta.braves.mlb.com/atl/history/story_of_the_braves.jsp.

[66] http://www.nba.com/hawks/history/season-by-season-recaps.html

[67] http://mercedesbenzstadium.com/ http://atlanta.braves.mlb.com/atl/ballpark/ suntrust-park/overview/ballpark/.

[68] http://www.bizjournals.com/birmingham/stories/2003/04/28/story3.html.

[69] http://www.atlanta-airport.com/fifth/atl/Airport_History.aspx.

[70] http://www.bizjournals.com/birmingham/stories/2003/04/28/story3.html.

[71] http://www.atlanta-airport.com/fifth/atl/Airport_History.aspx.

[72] http://www.georgiaencyclopedia.org/articles/counties-cities-neighborhoods/atlanta.

[73] http://www.bizjournals.com/atlanta/news/2013/04/25/martas-new-five-year-fiscal-plan-sees.html.

[74] http://www.olympic.org/atlanta-1996-summer-olympics.

[75] http://nces.ed.gov/pubs2002/2002114.pdf.

[76] http://data.bls.gov/timeseries/LASST130000000000003.

[77] http://www.redandblack.com/uganews/college-graduates-may-delay-careers-facing-today-s-job-market/article_fafb65c2-fcbd-11e3-8349-001a4bcf6878.html.

[78] https://cew.georgetown.edu/wp-content/uploads/2014/11/Recovery2020.ES_.Web_.pdf.

[79] http://www.census.gov/2010census/data/.

[80] https://ltgov.georgia.gov/college-and-career-academies.

[81] http://onlineathens.com/local-news/2013-08-03/career-academies-aim-build-workforce-give-sudents-head-start.

[82] http://georgiacareeracademies.org/?page_id=6.

[83] http://georgiacareeracademies.org/?page_id=6.

[84] http://onlineathens.com/local-news/2013-08-03/career-academies-aim-build-workforce-give-sudents-head-start.

[85] Albert Einstein, "Atomic Education Urged by Einstein," *New York Times* (25 May 1946).

[86] https://www.motorola.com/us/consumers/about-motorola-us/About_Motorola-History-Timeline/About_Motorola-History-Timeline.html#1980; Alexander Graham Bell, *booklet* (*Halifax, Nova Scotia: Maritime Telegraph & Telephone Ltd.*, 1979) 8.

[87] http://venturebeat.com/2015/12/10/9-things-you-may-not-know-about-the-mobile-marketing-landscape-and-should.

[88] http://www.nasa.gov/mission_pages/apollo/apollo11.html.

[89] http://www.forbes.com/powerful-brands/list/.

[90] http://appleinsider.com/articles/15/10/28/apple-rd-spending-hit-81b-in-2015-suggests-continued-work-on-massive-project.

[91] http://www.macobserver.com/article/2001/05/07.10.shtml.

[92] https://www.google.com/about/company/history/.

[93] https://www.google.com/selfdrivingcar/.

[94] https://www.highbeam.com/doc/1G1-278884854.html

[95] http://clatl.com/atlanta/atlantas-taxi-industry-declares-war-on-uber-lyft/Content?oid=10295234.

[96] https://newsroom.uber.com/2015/11/uberhealth/.

[97] http://www.nytimes.com/2011/05/15/nyregion/uber-and-weeels-offer-car-services-by-phone-app.html?_r=2.

[98] https://www.gadoe.org/External-Affairs-and-Policy/AskDOE/Pages/Schools-and-Districts.aspx.

[99] http://datacenter.spps.org/uploads/SOTW_A_Nation_at_Risk_1983.pdf.

[100] http://datacenter.spps.org/uploads/SOTW_A_Nation_at_Risk_1983.pdf, http://www.air.org/resource/three-decades-education-reform-are-we-still-nation-risk.

[101] http://www.peachpundit.com/2012/06/16/jobs-recovery-a-tale-of-two-georgias/.

[102] http://www.usatoday.com/story/news/nation/2015/04/01/atlanta-schools-cheating-scandal-verdict/70780606/.

[103] http://www.csmonitor.com/USA/Education/2011/0705/America-s-biggest-teacher-and-principal-cheating-scandal-unfolds-in-Atlanta.

[104] http://www.atlantada.org/pr_032913-1.php.

[105] http://www.ajc.com/news/news/local-education/atlanta-public-schools-wins-charter-status/nnnwY/.

[106] http://www.presidency.ucsb.edu/ws/index.php?pid=9455.

[107] Joyce Appleby and Terence Ball, *Jefferson: Political Writings* (New York: Cambridge University Press, 1999).

[108] https://www.gadoe.org/Curriculum-Instruction-and-Assessment/Assessment/Pages/CRCT.aspx

[109] https://www.gadoe.org/Curriculum-Instruction-and-Assessment/Assessment/Pages/CRCT.aspx.

[110] https://www.khanacademy.org/about.

[111] http://www.theguardian.com/education/2013/apr/23/sal-khan-academy-tutored-educational-website.

[112] http://www.theguardian.com/education/2013/apr/23/sal-khan-academy-tutored-educational-website.

[113] http://www.gatesfoundation.org/How-We-Work/Quick-Links/GrantsDatabase/Grants/2010/10/OPP1025663.

[114] Allan R. Odden, *Improving Student Learning When Budgets Are Tight* (Thousand Oaks, CA: Corwin, A SAGE Co., 2012).

[115] http://www.gavirtualschool.org/.

[116] http://www.calhounschools.org/Page/2395.

[117] http://www.alplm.org/272viewessay.aspx?id=619.

[118] http://www.forbes.com/sites/erikaandersen/2013/05/31/21-quotes-from-henry-ford-on-business-leadership-and-life/.

[119] http://www.reaganfoundation.org/reagan-quotes-detail.aspx?tx=2279.